The Police

THE POLICE

Ben Whitaker

CHIEF OF THE POLICE: If I die, the attempt will fail.
Order must be restored; traffic flow, jaywalkers must
be crushed.

The Balcony

Eyre & Spottiswoode

LONDON

First published 1964
Copyright © Ben Whitaker 1964
*Published simultaneously by Penguin
Books Ltd., Harmondsworth, Middlesex
Printed in Great Britain by
Billing & Sons Ltd., Guildford and London*

Contents

5

DIAGRAMS

Author's Acknowledgements

I am very grateful to many police officers of every rank in forces all over the country for 'assisting me in my inquiries', together with others at the Home Office, Scotland Yard, and the English and Scottish Police Federations. None of them, of course, necessarily associates himself with the ideas or opinions of this book. I would particularly like to thank the chief constable who helped me by distributing a lengthy questionnaire among his force. So many people are not allowed to be, or have asked not to be, named that it seems invidious to mention any individually; nevertheless I thank them all sincerely for their patience and help which made this book possible. Perhaps one day an amusing symposium will be written by the people who are investigated about investigators.

I am also especially grateful to Miss Maureen Cain for contributing Chapters 5 and 6, which are based on twelve months she spent with a county and a city force; to London University for the help of their computer with statistical material; to Mr Lawrence Dowdall amongst others for assisting on several points concerning the Scottish police; to Mr Millett Wood, Mr and Mrs Merfyn Turner, Mr David Napley, Mr William Hemming, Mr Arthur Deeks, and Mr Michael Walker for their help; and to Mr Eryl Hall-Williams and Mr William Mostyn-Owen among others for kindly reading the manuscript. I acknowledge also the kind permission of the Controller of H.M.S.O. to reprint as an appendix the Home Office Circular No. 31/1964. 'Judges' Rules and Administrative Directions to the Police', which is Crown Copyright.

The Royal Commission

There is a new readiness in Britain today to take a fresh look at institutions which we have long taken for granted. Among them are the police, who are a microcosm of some of the more intractable and interesting problems of human society. This book, whose own shortcomings as a scientific study will be readily apparent, is a plea that public opinion about the police and their problems should be better informed with evidence and understanding, instead of being spasmodically inflamed by cycles of ephemeral incidents. Often in the past the most vital questions in Britain have not been assessed dispassionately or scientifically, but viewed instead in the flickering light of various pressure groups or else in a rosy glow of historical sentiment. When public interest is aroused, it tends to concern itself more with superficial scapegoats, such as Sheffield or Rachman, than with the real underlying problems of the police or housing.

A witness before the 1929 Royal Commission on Police Powers and Procedure said:

> To represent the English police as the one unaltered element of the national life is to talk without meaning. When the times change, *all* men change with them. So many of both the friends and the critics of the police talk as if police constables were not men.

Policemen (like criminals) must be studied not as a

group but as individuals, not in isolation but in society, furthermore in the particular society that is British. It is one of the priceless attributes of this society that a book which contains frank criticisms as well as suggestions for improving the police can be written freely. To whitewash some aspects would be to insult the high standards that the majority of policemen hold.

A large part of the material of this book comes from the mouths of police officers of all ranks, who consider themselves to be one of the least heard sectors of the community. The Social Survey which was undertaken by the Central Office of Information for the Willink Commission in 1960 (whose results many policemen say they could not believe and still find difficulty in accepting) showed the opaqueness of the views that they and the public have of each other. For example, 69 per cent of policemen who were asked believed that the public's opinion of them had changed for the worse in recent years, compared with 2 per cent who thought it had improved; whereas when the public were questioned, very nearly twice as many people said that both their own feelings towards the police and the police's manner towards them had improved in that time as said the reverse. This defensive attitude on the part of policemen has unfortunate results: hypersensitivity to criticism makes those changes that are necessary harder to achieve, and some policemen who resent lack of understanding reciprocate by returning hostility for the hostility they imagine. The 1929 Royal Commission said that the main question which faced them was 'to find means to restore the relationship between the police and the public'. In 1960 another Royal Commission attempted to tackle this same problem, but the resulting new Police Bill does not provide any solution. This is one difficulty which is unlikely to be solved by inertia: unless remedies are found, the cleavage is more likely to widen than to disappear as urbanization and motoring increase in the future. If this book can help the public and the police to understand each other's viewpoints better, it will have achieved its purpose.

The traditional British remedy for a problem is to set up some form of committee. Six Parliamentary Commissions sat between 1770 and 1828 to inquire into the state of London's police. 'They were mainly appointed as a result of alarm after some particular crime or disturbance, and their recommendations, though by no means comprehensive or radical, were lost sight of as soon as the alarm subsided,' comments Mrs Hart in *The British Police*, and this description applies to much of the subsequent history. Since the First World War, no fewer than 54 further Committees have sat on different aspects of police questions. The genesis of the two most far-ranging, those under Lord Lee and Sir Henry Willink, was curiously similar: they originated fortuitously out of minor London cases. The first was set up in 1928 as a result of Parliamentary agitation about two incidents concerning a Miss Savidge and a Major Sheppard, which had happened to take place within the Metropolitan area – the only police district about which M.P.s could ask questions. Likewise in 1959, although there had been far graver events concerning the police in Cardiganshire, Brighton, Worcester, and Nottingham – during which people wondered how many other skeletons lay in cupboards that the Inspectors of Constabulary regularly certified were empty – it was not until the comparatively smaller Garratt-Eastmond case took place in the Metropolitan area that Mr Butler conceded to M.P.s a new Royal Commission.

Its fifteen members sat for two and a half years, compared with the eight members of the 1929 Lee Commission on Police Powers and Procedure who produced a unanimous and pungent Report (few of whose recommendations have been implemented) within seven months of the traditional 'Greeting' going to the busy if 'trusty and well-beloved' members. It is doubtful whether large commissions are the best means of untying difficult knots. Whatever their value for placating M.P.s, they have neither the time nor the resources to do any constructive research. Roots and facets of correlated problems frequently fail to be examined because they lie outside the terms of reference. The commission's corporate views tend either to be compromises, vaguely general, or conflicting. The 1962 Report, with ten members signing various dissents besides a Minority Report, has been criticized as being all three. Apart from the long overdue pay increase, its recommendations aroused little enthusiasm: tinkering, even where justified, has few admirers. It is significant that more copies of the Interim Report dealing with pay were sold than of the Final Report. *The Economist* called the latter 'frankly disappointing'. The Professor of Jurisprudence at London University said: 'Those who adopt the view that complacency as to themselves and their institutions is the besetting sin of the inhabitants of this island will find ample endorsement for that opinion in the tone, the arguments, and the findings of the Royal Commission on the Police 1962'; while a critic in *Public Law* in a detailed commentary called it

> unrealistic, glamourized, and too general . . . We are constantly being taken back into the past for which the Commission has great respect; and unless careful, we are mesmerized by verbiage and hollow phrases. . . . Members of the Commission, and especially the Chairman, spoke at

far too great length, instead of eliciting information from witnesses. Further, almost every time a witness referred to a particular happening, the Commission was reluctant to hear about it. But how else can a picture of what in fact happens in bad cases be built up? . . . Far too much time is taken up with explaining why things are as they are: for instance, why the legal position is uncertain and confusing. This is a largely pointless activity for a Royal Commission.

The Chairman was a former Conservative M.P. and barrister – neither innovationary occupations – but more serious is that the Commission included among its many members no recognized scientist, accountant, or expert in efficiency. In contrast to the Gowers Commission, for example, which made extensive researches here and abroad and produced a valuable textbook on capital punishment, the Willink Report made no permanent contribution to its subject. It includes literary quotations from Wordsworth and Johnson, but (apart from the figures on pay and public opinion) no scientific evidence other than from groups with a vested interest in the *status quo*. It is a major defect of reform by Commission that only such groups have the resources or the access to information which are necessary to be able to present a proper case.

Unlike Gowers, the Willink Commission appears to have heard no foreign opinion at all (other than Dr Goodhart's), yet international experience, readily attainable through Interpol, would have been particular valuable in taking the most fundamental decision with which it was faced: whether we should have a national force. There is much which could be learnt by comparing, for example, the workings of the national forces of Ireland, Denmark, Norway, or Holland with the dual national and local forces of France, Germany, or Sweden, and the Federal and local organizations in Canada or the United

States. No scientific attempt was made to measure the effect of our own present system of fragmented forces upon the efficiency of our police although this is essential before any decision about their future organization can be taken. Neither was there any assessment of how their effectiveness might be improved, other than by the panacea of a pay increase which, by the time the Final Report was written, the crime figures must have made evident was not enough.

Although the accountability of the police was one of their main terms of reference and also their *raison d'être*, the Commission failed to collect any national evidence of either the disciplinary charges or the criminal convictions against policemen. The Commission expressed anxiety about some social questions such as the attitudes of young people towards the police, but does not appear to have heard any evidence about them. The Survey also revealed that many police said that coloured people had grown more resentful of them recently: there is no sign that the Commission investigated this, or considered whether the fact that there is still not one coloured professional policeman in Britain might have any relevance.

Most criticized of all has been the Commission's interpretation of the findings of the Social Survey. These were available to them over a year before the Final Report was written, and it disclosed, for example, that 42·4 per cent of the public thought that some policemen took bribes, 34·7 per cent that the police used unfair methods to get information, 32 per cent that they might distort evidence in court, and 17·8 per cent that on occasions they used too much force. The number of people questioned who said they had a personal knowledge of serious misconduct by a policeman within the last ten years is equivalent throughout the country to 65,000 cases per annum, which is nearly one per police officer every year. The conclusion of the Royal Commission, however, was:

> (para. 338) The findings of the survey constitute an over-whelming vote of confidence in the police. . . . We therefore assert confidently, on the basis of this survey, that relations between the police and the public are on the whole very good, and we have no reason to suppose that they have ever, in recent times, been otherwise. This is a finding which we believe will give great satisfaction to Your Majesty, to the police, and to the public.

> (para. 350) A study of this valuable report reveals an attitude of mind on both sides that augurs well for the con-tinuance of good relations between the police and the public for years to come.

The police themselves – and it is much to their credit – did not share this complacency. 69 per cent felt there was a need for an inquiry into their relations with the public, and 89 per cent wanted measures taken to improve their relations with the public and gave suggestions for doing so. The Report of the Survey concluded:

> This survey showed that the police felt that a change for the worse had occurred in relations between themselves and the public, and were deeply disturbed by it. The reasons given for this change reflect police anxiety not only about the attitudes and behaviour of certain sections of the public, but also over some aspects of police organization.

The views of the members of the public who were inter-viewed differed sharply on many questions from those of the police. For example, 21·5 per cent of the public thought that the standard of people who enter the police now had improved, compared with 12·5 per cent who thought it was worse: whereas only 12·6 per cent of the police thought it showed improvement, compared with 51·9 per cent who thought the reverse. For some reason which is not easily apparent the Commission seems to have ignored the police's views in favour of the public's whenever they were in conflict; although each policeman interviewed is both trained to observe and report and in daily touch with the public, whereas many of the members of the public, who were chosen at random, may well have had little or no recent contact with any policeman. The sample taken of the public was also unsatisfactory through having been drawn from the electoral roll, and also because, although no one younger than 18 was questioned, the younger age groups between that age and 39 were under-represented: e.g. the 18–21 age group formed only 3·8 per cent of the sample, compared with 6·4 per cent of the total population of the country.

The Commission, unable to obtain national figures as to whether, for example, complaints about the police are increasing or not, leaned heavily on the abstractions contained in the Survey. But the purpose of a Social Survey is to gather opinion, not facts, and it is no substitute for genuine research. It is surprising that the Commission never compared the public's allegations of serious police misconduct either with actual statistics, or by asking the police themselves who were surveyed any questions as to their knowledge of corruption, perjury, or violence. The impression this omission gives – that on this important question the evidence of police officers is rejected in favour of the views of a tiny section of the public (many of them no doubt based on hearsay or gained from the press) – is an odd one. The opinions of all the lawyers' associations which gave evidence before the Commission, comprising people whose job keeps them in contact with relations between the police and the public, were unanimous in supporting the disquiet expressed by the police themselves.

Hardest to understand of all is the attitude which is common throughout the Report, and most clearly revealed when the majority (with the honourable exceptions of Lord Geddes, Leslie Hale, and Alastair Hetherington) gave their reason for rejecting independent inquiries into complaints, 'because the appearance of greater justice to the public is liable to be bought at the expense of the police'. Quite apart from the confusion which seems to be implied in this statement as to just which body is maintained for the benefit of the other, it is astonishing that there should be thought to be any distinction, let alone conflict, between public justice and police efficiency. Any policeman will say that the effectiveness of the force depends primarily on the help and goodwill of the public. The respect of the public and the morale of the police are therefore not incompatible but indivisible. The Willink Report, while making many admirable suggestions for improvements of detail, seems to be permeated with a fear of worrying the morale of the force. The Commission failed to realize that this morale depends, not on words, but on two vital contributions which neither the Report nor the new Police Bill supply: first, their greater efficiency, and secondly their closer rapport with the public.

CHAPTER I

Police: Force or Service?

Before attempting to examine the present efficiency of our police and any ways by which it might be improved, it is necessary to consider what their role is in our changing society: what, in fact, are the police for?

At first sight it seems a strange idea for sheep to pay some of their number to dress as sheepdogs; and it is interesting to speculate how a country might be if it did not have any policemen. There is a traditional British reluctance to admit the necessity for professional policemen, perhaps for the same historical reasons as we prefer amateur M.P.s. Many people still like to describe the policeman as only a professional citizen – a man paid to perform, as duty, acts which he might have done voluntarily. Historically, this was his origin: those citizens, particularly among the new mercantile classes, who were nominated to act for a year as the unpaid and unpopular parish constable increasingly used to contract out of their duty of law-enforcement by paying a substitute (who was often as useless as Elbow in *Measure for Measure*). When this system demonstrated its futility by many hundred deaths in the Gordon Riots of 1780, and the Peterloo massacre shortly afterwards showed the dangers of using the military, Peel's 'New Police' in 1829 made a fresh professional start.

Its form was shaped by Colonel Charles Rowan and Richard Mayne (a thirty-two year old barrister), the two

Irishmen who were the Commissioners for its first twenty-
one years. Their instructions to the first Metropolitan
policemen were based on the realization by the reforming
magistrate Sir Patrick Colquhoun that a preventive uniformed branch was as necessary as the 'Criminal Investigation Department' of the Fieldings' thief-takers. Their
original words are used today in teaching police recruits
their role:

> The primary object of an efficient police is the prevention
> of crime; the next that of detection and punishment of
> offenders if crime is committed. . . . It should be understood
> at the outset that the object to be attained is the prevention
> of crime. To this great end every effort of the police is
> directed. The security of person and property, the preserva-
> tion of the public tranquility, and all other objects of a
> police establishment will thus be better effected than by the
> detection and punishment of the offender after he has
> succeeded in committing the crime. . . . Every member of
> the Force must remember that his duty is to protect and help
> members of the public no less than to apprehend guilty
> persons. Consequently, while prompt to prevent crime and
> to arrest criminals, he must look upon himself as a servant
> and guardian of the general public and treat all law-
> abiding citizens, irrespective of their social position, with
> unfailing patience and courtesy.

To the primary question 'What are the police *for*?' this
is a useful rough and ready answer. But the criminal law
which the police exist to implement is not an abstract set
of immutable rules. The laws and the way they are applied
reflect the values of the society that can both create and
annul them. Thus in a democratic society the right of the
individual to life, liberty, and property is highly prized.
The social value which the English place on, for example,
freedom from arbitrary arrest, freedom from police intru-
sion into their homes, freedom even from the witness-box

is enormous. Yet, as the words of Mayne suggest, the other values of security of person and property can be protected only by means of preventing those who hold anti-social values from expressing them. (And what is anti-social today may not be so tomorrow, or even today as between different social groups in the population.) To the criminal law, society delegates the task of protecting its values, or at least the values that are held by those who have the power to legislate. To the police, society delegates the irreconcilable tasks of enforcing the law by means which, if they are to be effective, must necessarily infringe the principles that the law protects.

There is a paradox here: we need law enforced, but some say not over efficiently. The curious position over the admissibility of evidence that has been illegally obtained illustrates ways of resolving the paradox. Evidence found during an unlawful search is not admissible in an American Federal court of law. The argument is clear: it is not considered right to admit evidence which is obtained by exceeding the compromise position that society has set between liberty and law enforcement. On the other hand, whether obtained lawfully or unlawfully, evidence, after all, remains evidence, and the social good of law enforcement has in England tipped the scales the other way: tangible evidence obtained by unlawful means may nonetheless be admissible evidence under English law.

On the one hand, today, we value efficiency and demand results; on the other we suspect strong authority and defend the rights of the individual more than ever before. We ask the police, as the agents of force necessary even in a peacetime democratic society, to fulfil many of our responsibilities which we acknowledge to be essential, if unpleasant. But we also use their uniforms as the most readily identifiable targets for our resentment at these same tasks. Behind the discussion in this book, of rights of the community and of the individual, lies a clash of values that is inevitable when we place policemen in this crossfire. At each point the conflict must be resolved by assessing the interests at stake: each reader can make up his own mind in the light of his own social values.

There is a further modern answer to the question 'What are the police for?' Most members of the public today encounter the policeman as some form of traffic regulator, which was certainly not the case in 1829. Behind the increase in of police activity nowadays lies a profound shift in society's use of the criminal law and thus of the police. Certain public standards are needed to keep a highly industrialized and over-populated society alive; we have made the enforcement of those standards the concern of the criminal law and thus of the police in a range of what are sometimes called 'public welfare offences'. As Professor Friedmann has written in *Law in a Changing Society*:

> It is clear that, as a group, this type of offence, while going under the general label of criminal law, is of an essentially different character from the criminal offences based on individual wrongdoing. Like all law, the conditions under which criminal liability is imposed depend upon a balance of values in a given society. Even the innocent killing of a man harms the society, but the law generally considers that a severe penalty for murder or manslaughter should not be imposed, except on proof of individual guilt. Public welfare offences are, by contrast, essentially standardized. In the balance of values, it is generally considered more essential that violations of traffic rules or food laws should be strictly punished, in the interests of the public, rather than that the degree of individual guilt should be measured in each case. ... Attacks against the spread of the strict liability principle

for this type of offence have often been based on the ground that the imposition of a relatively small fine, e.g. for the operation of dangerous machinery or the sale of injurious drugs, is in any case no adequate sanction. Such criticism seems to misconceive the essentially different character of the sanction imposed in these cases. The purpose is to impose certain standards of conduct in the interest of the community at large. . . .

Detailed examination of the use of police time for traffic and other public welfare offences must, therefore, be seen against the social needs of the kind of society which we have chosen to create.

The clash between the social values of liberty and law enforcement and the twentieth-century shift in the uses of the criminal law, and consequently of the police, together show how perceptive Mayne and Rowan were when they recognized that any real power that the force would have depended not on extra laws but on the cooperation of the public. How vital this relationship was they appreciated from the outset: the police were told they must cultivate it by 'combining modesty and firmness, and dignity of manner and address, with good humour and kindly friendliness, and by showing infinite patience under provocation'.[1]

A further result which had not been anticipated was that society increasingly transferred many other responsibilities to the police. In the same way as Tudor M.P.s had passed the supervision of apprentices and vagrants on to their constables (whose office was older than Parliament itself), modern governments have employed policemen to be their agents in Acts of Parliament which range from aliens and diseased animals to issuing certificates for firearms. In

---

[1] C. Reith: *A Short History of the British Police* (O.U.P., 1948).

addition, the police acquired the major task of having to control traffic because of their general duty to protect life and property. Nevertheless the idea that a constable is only a citizen supporting the πολις – perhaps the crux of Dr Goodhart's disagreement with the other members of the Commission – dies hard.[1]

Policemen have always been very anxious to keep civilian roots. They like to wear civilian clothes whenever possible, which is part of the reason there is always a waiting-list of men to transfer to the C.I.D., despite the slower promotion and the enormous unpaid overtime. 64 per cent of officers who were questioned[2] said that they prefer to live among the public rather than with other policemen in segregated quarters. A wish for recruits to have as much civilian experience as possible is why many police officers advocate a high age of entry, and prefer the proportion of cadets (who are trained as police from school-leaving age) to be kept to a minority. Although the increasing competition of outside jobs is causing a gradual erosion of this policy, the Police Federation[3] told the Royal Commission that there 'could be nothing more disastrous for relationships between police and public' than to make the police a profession. As their work grows increasingly

[1] Our fear of a despotic élite remains in the pejorative associations of the tautologous phrase 'police state'; hence bus-loads of policemen wait in side streets rather than intimidate demonstrators by a show of strength.

[2] The survey whose percentage findings are quoted throughout this book was carried out in a large county force in England (whose area covers both urban and rural communities) during November 1963.

[3] The respective Federations of England and Scotland are the police equivalents of trades unions for all ranks below superintendents and chief officers (who each have their own association), although they are forbidden to affiliate with the T.U.C. Fewer than 0.5 per cent of police officers exercise their right to opt out of the Federation.

technical, training will inevitably lengthen and become more specialized; but the police are no exception to that nostalgia for the amateur which Anthony Sampson found in every bone of Britain.

The truer descendant of the civilian policeman or Anglo-Saxon *tythingman* is the part-time Special constable, who is unpaid except for his out-of-pocket expenses. By an Act of Charles II in 1673, any citizen could be summoned to be sworn in as one, and heavily fined if he refused: this law was still in force just before the Second World War when the Hartlepool Magistrates tried to enrol an unwilling transport driver, to cries of 'Press Gang'. But today only volunteers are employed. They used to wear armbands but now have the normal blue uniform distinguishable only by a flat cap and the initials 'S.C.'

Besides being used in war-time as replacements for regulars who joined up, Specials were also frequently employed against agitators, from the times of the Chartists down to the 226,300 Special constables who joined at the time of the General Strike. This gave them an unfortunate political connotation: members of Hurlingham Polo Club could be seen dressed in their kit of boots, spurs, and topees cantering off to fresh sport swinging their riding crops. The following incident recounted by an ex-Special in R. Seth's *The Specials* helps to show why they are still treated with some suspicion.

> Wakefield was out in a flash leading the scrum to victory. He crashed open the door with such force that when I reached it – about third – the poor little fellow who had been acting as sentry and using the keyhole to watch through was still up against the wall unconscious, with a lump the size of an orange between his eyes.
>
> Upstairs in a bare room furnished only with a table and a few upright chairs we found a pathetic-looking bunch of

'workers' sitting round the table, turning off 'subversive literature' on an old Roneo. The walls were decorated with Communist posters, and on the mantelpiece was a plaster bust of Lenin. We smashed the Roneo, disconnected the telephone, and bundled the lot into the lorries en route for the Yard. Happy days! Though looking back, I can't help feeling it was all much more of a tragedy than the joyride it appeared to be to us.

Special constables now include a much broader representation of the population. Scotland today has 7,700 and England and Wales 51,000, of whom about 25 per cent are regularly employed. This is only half the authorized total, and their number has decreased by about a thousand in each of the last two years. In Scotland their use is forbidden except for emergencies, but the Metropolitan area is so undermanned that there they are welcomed by most regulars because they enable them to get a Sunday off by taking over duties on that day. (The Metropolitan policeman at present only gets one Sunday free in four – and that is sometimes cancelled: it is particularly precious because it is the only day on which all his family can be together.) 30 per cent of regular policemen who were questioned in 1963 said that they thought Specials should only be used for crowd control, 28 per cent for traffic control, and 4 per cent for election duties. Some regulars replied, 'Most of the time they are a burden to us,' and 'without them, our conditions would have improved years ago.'

The fact that both the regular and special policeman is as subject to law as anybody else is one of the reasons why people are anxious that allegations against him should be investigated fully and impartially. A policeman has, in fact, few legal rights that the ordinary citizen does not possess, and outside his own and any adjoining police area he has only the same status as anyone else. An interesting illustration of his position occurs when a police-car is pursuing criminals: the police driver may exceed the speed limit, but he is liable for an accident in the same way as a private driver and can be prosecuted for dangerous driving. Most people will agree that this is the correct perspective, because, in the words of the Metropolitan Commissioner, 'it is not right to jeopardize lives even when chasing bank-robbers'.

The fact that our police do not carry arms is another result of this attitude: we have no force like the French armed *gardes* or *gens d'armes*. This makes our police dependent on persuasion and public goodwill – one reason why it is vital for them to have excellent relations with the public. Although they are trained in unarmed combat, and male officers carry a 'stick' for extra confidence in a special pocket down the right-hand trouser leg, neither is often used. There has been no baton- or horse-charge, of the kind used against the hunger marchers, since the Second World War. Despite the number of assaults on the police having trebled in the last twenty years, no policeman who was questioned wanted to be armed. 66 per cent who were asked gave as their reason that criminals would also arm; others said that it would damage their relations with the public. For special assignments policemen can have a firearm on request: they do so, in fact, on only about ten occasions a year; more are offered but refused. In the United States (where recruits are trained in decision-making by firing at cinema screens) 71 policemen are killed a year – including an average of four in New York compared with about one every four years in London.

The new Police Bill has increased the penalty for assault upon a policeman; though it is debatable whether the punishment for assaulting any man should be different from that for assaulting another – especially as, under our present law, knowledge that a man in plain clothes was a policeman is not necessary for conviction. It might be preferable if all assaults were penalized more heavily, so that the law protected persons as strongly as it protects property. But the special penalty undoubtedly gives the police greater confidence in their dangerous life: on or off duty, a policeman is assumed to be ready to risk his life rescuing the drowning or burning, or tackling an armed man or a rabid dog.[1] The police exerted pressure to be included in a special category under the Homicide Act – although Dr Sellin has now shown in a study that fewer policemen proportionally are killed in those U.S. States which have abolished capital punishment than in those which still retain it.

There are two separate branches in the regular police force: the Uniformed, and the Criminal Investigation Department. The vast majority of the public never encounter any C.I.D. men, who account for only 9 per cent of the total strength. More of the Uniformed branch's time is spent assisting people in various ways than in dealing with crime. Policemen themselves, when asked what they consider their job to be, often talk in phrases – generally learnt in their training – such as 'the protection of life' or 'helping children and old people'. 16 per cent of men who were asked what they like most about police life replied,

---

[1] About forty policemen were injured on duty in each week of 1963, including one member of the Manchester City Police who, called to the aid of a strip-tease artiste whose boa-constrictor had escaped, was bitten when he found it under a bed. Mr Frank Norman said in *The Police and the Public*: 'I reckon it is just about the last job I would ever take even if I was starving to death.'

'the sense of giving service to the public'. 40 per cent mentioned 'the variety' and 'meeting people'.[1] Many policemen still do extra voluntary work, particularly in youth clubs. Some older policemen regret the change in their relationship with the public brought about by the end of their responsibility for fire and ambulance services.

Although urban forces have tended to be swamped by the two problems of traffic and the protection of premises, a police officer in a rural district is still more concerned with poachers and poultry thieves, or dealing with out-breaks of fire or animal disease: when foot-and-mouth occurs, a twenty-four hour guard on the gate is necessary. One village constable said that eighteen families regularly bring him their income-tax forms to fill in, besides looking on him as their doctor, marriage counsellor, and general adviser. Some of the duties, for instance acting as a father figure to women and children, may be personally satis-fying: others such as being present at the eviction of tenants may be distasteful; but a policeman is not allowed to have any public feelings. Although his oath as a con-stable is to serve the Crown and not the local authority, he is often also asked to execute the rate-payers' wishes – by, for instance running beatniks out of a Cornish town, or urging gypsies and tramps on to neighbouring districts. The days when a chief constable employed a policeman as his batman or for digging in his garden are gone, but in at least one borough the washing of councillors' cars continues. Not many members of the public are aware

[1] 24 per cent mentioned comradeship, 16 per cent interest, 10 per cent security, 8 per cent pride in doing a worthwhile job, 8 per cent doing an open-air job, 4 per cent being looked up to by the public. One man answered 'having carried out prosecutions without malice'.

that they can hire a policeman for a private function: in the Metropolitan area, for example, a P.C. costs 16s. 6d. (a police woman 13s. 6d.) or a C.I.D. chief superintendent 36s. 4d. an hour, plus 30s. for 'morning or evening dress', 21s. 6d. for a horse, or 18s. for a dog.

Since the policeman in his job suffers from acting as a battlefield for the tension between state and individual, conflict situations are inescapable in his work. Different viewpoints lead to varying opinions as to what makes a good police officer, just as in the armed forces men and officers often mean something different when they talk of a 'good N.C.O.'. One constable said that he regarded himself as the agent of the law, another saw himself as the servant of the public and not of the state, while a third described himself as the 'agent of the established order since laws are always made in their favour'. Many policemen in the last war understood that if we were invaded their duty was to stay in the invaded area and care for the people, rather than to fight or withdraw: presumably this would be their function if the country were ever divided by a civil war.

In their position, it is obviously essential for the police to be free of any suspicion of partiality – social, political, racial, or any other – even though they are part of a national society where prejudice and class influence are common. By their own Disciplinary Code they are prohibited from taking any active part in politics: they were not even allowed to vote in Parliamentary elections before 1887, or in local ones until 1893. Fortunately, outside a few local disputes such as at Nottingham in 1959, the police have never become a party political issue in this country. We do not suffer from what is called the 'numbers game' in the U.S.A., whereby a traffic violator will ask the cop for his number and mention his friend the Mayor.[1] Although political influence of this nature is unknown here, allegations have recently been made that certain groups are selected for prosecution, particularly on charges such as 'obstruction' where discretion is wide. When sellers of *Peace News* were prosecuted in Oxford, and Miss Pat Arrowsmith was prosecuted for holding a meeting in Bolton in 1963, they all protested that other people were allowed to act as they had done with impunity. A past Metropolitan Commissioner said that when he had complaints coming in from Fascists and Communists, he knew that his men were being impartial: but this is not necessarily true. The most impressive sight in London is to see the police marching in protection of a procession with those objects they have scant sympathy. But in a few recent cases when some demonstrators have been treated in a totally different way from others, an impression has been given that a decision has been taken at a high level for meetings advocating certain opinions to receive less toleration. Exceptionally vehement measures appear to have been taken against those who demonstrated about Greek political prisoners in 1963. Many people find it difficult to understand why the police should prevent people from entering the Mall to protest peacefully about one queen (especially when the Prime Minister had given an undertaking in the House that demonstrations would be allowed), while much larger crowds are never considered an obstruction of the same highway on other royal occasions.

Policemen themselves are fully aware how important it is for them not even to be suspected of any bias. They are

[1] 'I know that my man is going to make a good police chief,' one Mayor of Indianapolis said, 'because he has been my tailor for twenty years.'

indignant when a titled landowner or a magistrate or alderman is not prosecuted for driving offences within his own area. They are probably less socially influenced than some lay magistrates, who in a recent study were shown to be relatively severer when, for instance, sentencing a working-class man in a middle-class district.

Different social classes make use of the police in varying ways: working-class people, although often still generally hostile, take their personal problems to a respected individual policeman in a way a middle-class person would not. The situation in the past, when policemen were expected to be deferential and polite to landowners while stern but paternal to their farm-workers, has been radically altered – especially by the motoring laws, which have unkindly included many of the former in the largest criminal class of all. Nevertheless they are still likely to be addressed: 'Excuse me, sir', whereas a motor-cyclist will hear 'Hey, you'. In the Social Survey, 24·1 per cent of the public said they thought that the 'upper classes, rich or influential people' were inclined to receive preferential treatment, although only 5·6 per cent said they had personal knowledge of such cases. But on the other hand one P.C. said that he never prosecuted anybody as meticulously as the woman driver who began 'My son works in the Home Office . . .', and at least one chief constable has given strict orders that 'any offender attempting to swing the "I was dining with the chief constable last night" line is to be jumped on'.

It would be fascinating to study in university towns whether the same offence receives different treatment from police and magistrates, according to being described as an 'undergraduate prank' or 'delinquent hooliganism'. Certainly tenants in the St Stephen's Gardens area of Paddington must have felt surprised to read that over 50 police officers could be spared recently for a case of property stolen from a member of the royal family, when not one person was convicted for intimidation during three years' terror of violence in their own area.

Much of the resentment of the police in some districts (such as those parts of London and South Wales where they are still booed on the cinema screen) dates from the time of the hunger marches. It is diminishing (old songs like 'We'll kill all the coppers who come down our way' have disappeared) but many mothers still teach their children to fear a policeman by using him as a threat for misbehaviour. Some working people tend to mistrust policemen, for 'always watching. and being the agents of 'Them'. One policeman said: 'My own experience of political demonstrators confirms that this attitude still exists and is fully used by unscrupulous public elements to arouse strong feelings. The inability of the police to express political opinions adds to the impression that they're on the side of the establishment.' In parts of Liverpool and some housing estates in north-west England, the police live like a race apart – occasionally in almost siege conditions with their windows being broken twice a year. In these areas the policeman can be an isolated figure, attempting to advocate middle-class values of restraint and behaviour, such as the channelling of aggression into social anbition. Many policemen originate from lower social and economic groups, but soon acquire the middle-class standards of obedience, cleanliness, and punctuality which are built into the police Disciplinary Code.

Today, it is difficult to believe that such a thing as a police strike could ever have happened in English history (in the same way as it is difficult to remember we were once a Republic, or Carson in Ulster, or the Abdication crisis). But in 1872 and 1890 some of the police went on strike for more pay, and in 1918 about 6,000 and in 1919 2,400 men came out asking for recognition of their union.[1] In 1926 the police refused to join the General Strike, although their situation was not an easy one and their feelings must have been mixed during some incidents. Afterwards *The Times* collected a public subscription of £242,000 in gratitude – a 'gargantuan tip' in the words of one chief inspector – but some policemen disliked it because it came from the upper classes and impugned their impartiality; and they wrote to the *Police Review* suggesting it should be given to people who needed it.

In judging what effect the police have on society, some people blame the police unfairly for laws which they did not make and may themselves dislike. (For this reason, they regard a campaign like 'Marples must go' as a welcome development.) It is not the police but parliamentary inertia and the public's lack of political interest which should be blamed for the fact that today, in 1964, a person can be sent to prison for fourteen years for wounding cattle, compared with only two years for cruelty to children; or that the maximum penalty for damaging hopbinds is fourteen years, whereas that for destroying any work of art, science, or literature is at most six months. Continual revision is needed to keep our statues in line with present-day values: many still reflect the proprietary and philistine values of their eighteenth- and nineteenth-century creators, preserved by our reverence for tradition.

[1] Although police strikes have now been made illegal, in 1963 all the Helsinki police officers are reported to have sent in their resignations on the same day.

However, the old Marxist attack on the police for preventing the redistribution of property is misconceived: it is more important that they and the rule of law make civilization possible by the prevention of violence. Criticism of the police and the prosecuting authorities for being arbiters of morals equally fails to recognize that they are forced to do so only by laws which meddle with morality. Under our legal system it is not the police but the juryman or magistrate who acts as the interpreter of morals.

It is true that in exercising their discretion the police assume a function which is quasi-judicial rather than executive – and one which can have a considerable effect. For example, in Manchester in 1955 there was only one prosecution for male importuning, none at all in 1956 or 1957, and only two in 1958. At the end of 1958 a new chief constable arrived, and prosecutions for this offence rose rapidly: from 30 in 1959 to 105 in 1960, 135 in 1961, and 216 in 1962. Apart from the local police area's policy, each station officer, when he weighs evidence to decide if there is a *prima facie* case and whether or not to accept a charge, has a role not far different from that of the continental examining magistrate. Both stages of the discretion whether to prosecute happen to be innocent of any legal authority, though naturally their exercise is the subject of few formal complaints. But the decisions involved can give rise to many other problems. An arrest or detention later judged to be illegal can involve the payment of heavy damages, and the policeman on duty has neither the time nor the law-books which are available to those who may later sue him. In making up his mind, he has to take account of the relative considerations of his own, the local Bench's, and a public jury's views, as well as the policy of his superior officers. Many policemen say that the most difficult part of their work is to know when to enforce the law and when to turn a half-closed eye. Since crimes are only certain acts 'believed to be socially harmful by a group of people which has power to enforce its beliefs', there are sometimes substantial minorities who disagree with measures. It is doubtful whether a majority of people in this country today approve of the law on abortion, Sunday observance, or licensing, although each is defended by politically powerful groups.

In the Metropolitan Police area in 1962, 768,555 traffic offences were dealt with by verbal warning and another 75,845 by a written caution (also without legal authority incidentally), compared with 183,504 which resulted in a summons. This discretion is not easy to distinguish from the power to impose an on-the-spot fine, which is often resisted on the grounds that the police and the judiciary have separate functions in this country. But frequently it is the apparent unfairness of being prosecuted or having their car towed away which is most resented by people who see others escaping with impunity. Sometimes they are irritated because they remember a different policy in the same street in the past, or cannot understand why night parking in exactly similar places requires lights in one city and not in another. The factors such as accident rates, varying perhaps at different times of any day or week, which influence the police's policy, and any alterations to the policy itself are rarely made known to the public. The impossibility of properly enforcing some regulations may well encourage a general disregard for the law by diminishing people's respect for the concept both of law and of themselves as law-abiding persons. Ineffectual restrictions cause harm by weakening natural self-enforced controls; they certainly have added to the

35

difficulties of the police. In the Social Survey, 91·4 per cent of the police questioned said they thought that the policeman's job of enforcing the law had become harder in recent years: 36·2 per cent because of traffic work, and 31·4 per cent because of increased legislation; besides others who mentioned their dislike of having to enforce unfair laws or ones against underprivileged people.

With the growth in the number of administrative offences, and the shortage of manpower which is compelling the police to give selective priorities to the enforcement of laws, the incidence of their discretion has increased. It also extends to more serious offences. In 1960, 13 per cent of all indictable offenders known to the police were cautioned – for a variety of reasons: perhaps because it was a first offence, or because there was too little evidence or because an employer was reluctant to prosecute. Some offenders escape prosecution by providing information about other criminals. Although police discretion in some cases is supplanting the function of Judges, it is often exercised for humane reasons. A few forces have a policy of warning children up to four or five times before bringing them to court. Some rigorously prosecute offences which are brought to light by blackmail, whereas others do not. One force, when a man lost his wife after twenty years of devoted marriage in a car accident for which he was acquitted for dangerous driving, then proceeded to prosecute him a second time for careless driving.

The two offences in which there is probably the greatest variation in prosecuting policy are abortion and homosexual behaviour. There are fewer than 100 prosecutions for abortion each year – under 0·1 per cent of the total estimated number. Only 24 per cent of policemen who were questioned in 1963 said that they thought abortion

36

should be a criminal offence. Enforcing the law about abortion discriminates in favour of the rich, and some police, particularly in poorer areas, have a certain amount of sympathy for the altruistic abortionist and tend to ignore his activities unless some tragedy or trouble occurs. Adult homosexuality is similarly connived at in some areas, whereas a mile away other officers act as *agents provocateurs*, or spend hours crouched in the broom-cupboards of public lavatories with their eye to holes bored in the door. A minority of policemen pursue homosexuals with an almost pathological ferocity: happily married fathers have been prosecuted for an offence committed years before when they were boys, which has come to light through a confession.

A more standard policy for some crimes is obtained through the office of the Director of Public Prosecutions, who takes charge in some 8 per cent of the most serious criminal cases. Many people would prefer an extension of his function so that all prosecuting decisions were removed from the hands of the police. This would not only lead to a more consistent policy for laws which are made nationally, but also save the police work and at the same time improve their relations with the public. Each offence would still receive individual consideration, but according to standard criteria instead of the varying idiosyncrasies of different chief constables and local authorities. (The chairman of one small borough's Watch Committee used to go through the chief constable's files each morning and tell him whom to prosecute.) In Scotland (from where England could learn on several legal matters) each court has a procurator-fiscal who decides on and conducts prosecutions, and who periodically meets with his colleagues in order to discuss policy. Critics of the present English system would also like all prosecutions to be brought in the name of the Crown instead of an individual police officer, and think that policemen should not be seen either conducting prosecutions or acting as ushers in courts. This might cause the expression 'police court' to die out in practice as well as in theory, as well as lead to a considerable saving of police manpower.

As a result of Parliament having made him an all-purpose public servant, a policeman is called upon to play a wide variety of parts. He needs the experience of an arbitrator, social worker, lawyer, and doctor, without being trained as any of them. A good policeman knows his limitations and when he should contact a specialist social worker (some policemen, for instance, take potential suicides to their local Samaritan branch). Because they are often the first public servants to come into contact with many social misfits and failures, it is highly important that they should be trained to be able to give advice and to classify cases correctly.

How is the role of the police likely to develop in the future? Their primary function, of which there is no sign of any withering away, will remain, in the American phrase, 'the maintenance of public order and the protection of persons and property from the hazards of public accidents and the commission of unlawful acts'. There will always be a need for the 'preventive medicine' of the sight of police uniforms and patrol cars. The deterrent effect they have has been studied on the continent: the stationing of a *gendarme* at a blind corner has been shown to reduce accidents, and it was reported that the Paris force in 1959, when many police were away in Algeria, successfully employed even cut-out dummies at dangerous cross-roads. After the Germans had deported the Danish police force in 1944, larceny and fraud (but not murder or sexual crimes) increased sharply. The value in this country of the presence of the man on the beat was shown in a recent experiment by the Metropolitan police, when one of their twenty-two divisions was brought up to its pre-war strength on the beat by borrowing 102 men. During the experimental period, indictable crimes in this division fell (breaking-in by 32 per cent), compared with the other divisions whose crimes showed an increase of 9·2 per cent over the previous year.

Before the last war, many policemen saw themselves as playing a 'cuff-on-the-ear' role against crime. A sergeant in a West Country force recounted how he regularly used to control gangs of unruly youths by 'setting upon them in the dark when there was not more than two of them together and giving them a good thumping'. But when in 1957 a police constable at Thurso gave 'a moderate cuff on the face' to a provocative fifteen-year-old boy, a Tribunal was later set up by both Houses of Parliament which heard evidence for six days and published a long report (under the motto *Nemo me impune lacessit*). The Waters case publicly discouraged such methods on the part of the police, although they continue to be used against poachers and are more tolerated in northern England. Some policemen are puzzled by the change in public opinion and ask why parents, teachers, and magistrates now have a lower threshold in their tolerance of physical violence.

94 per cent of policemen who were questioned in 1963 said that they thought they should not be concerned with the punishment of crime, although 18 per cent in answer to another question replied that they thought that lay

magistrates were too lenient. Sometimes policemen express outrage at certain crimes – especially those committed by sex-offenders (who also fall outside the pale of the prison community). In the past the police, like the majority of the general public, have been more interested in the methods of crime than its cause. One quite senior serving officer said that he thought that the Howard League for Penal Reform was responsible for the recent increase in offences. 'Policemen don't see that a term of imprisonment might do more harm', commented one stipendiary Magistrate. But an increasing number of policemen are now growing aware of the complexity of the problems of criminology. When London University started a three-year course in the subject in 1963, 800 police officers applied for the 100 places, and over 1,000 applied to join a similar course in Manchester.

The National Association of Probation Officers told the Royal Commission that since attendance centres had been introduced in 1948,

> where the police have been asked to take part in the organization or running of such centres, this has in many cases been used as an opportunity for preventive and constructive work, and for understanding by the police of the inherent possibilities of some apparently criminal young people. The end of a period of attendance has frequently been followed by continued interest by the police in the welfare of the young person, usually by a request to a probation officer to keep in touch with the lad or his family.

The best-known new development in the social work of the police is the Juvenile Liaison Officer scheme, launched by Liverpool in 1949 and since copied by some fifteen other forces in England and Wales and another six in Scotland (although this is only the organized form of work many individual policemen have always done on or off duty). Under the Liverpool plan, selected volunteer police officers do full-time duty supervising cautioned juveniles in liaison with their parents, school or youth club authorities, and the probation service. There are three basic conditions for supervision: (1) the child must admit the offence, which cannot be a grave one; (2) he must not have been in trouble previously; (3) his parents must give their consent. The juvenile liaison officer investigates his background and attempts to foster in the mind of the child ideas which will lead to responsible citizenship, and also, where necessary, to bring home to the parents their responsibilities. When he suspects that a child requires more specialized treatment, he hands the case over to the appropriate authority, i.e. school medical officer, child guidance clinic, or the psychiatric department of children's hospitals. If the juvenile liaison officer discovers another social agency is actively interested, he withdraws from the case. The idea for such schemes among the police seems to have grown from a wish to keep young people (the peak age for theft is fourteen) out of court: partly in order to avoid giving a child a criminal label at an early age, and partly because of dislike of the delays of the juvenile courts which have replaced the earlier cuff-on-the-ear methods. The policy is in reality only a more constructive extension of the power of discretion which the police have always possessed; but it has met with criticism because 42 per cent of the 818 children supervised at Liverpool in 1960, for example, had not yet committed any offence, but had been suggested by parents, teachers, or other policemen as 'potential delinquents'. J. A. Mack in a survey in the *British Journal of Criminology* has estimated that of the juveniles who have been supervised (four out of five of whom are boys) roughly 90 per cent are not known to have offended within the following three years.

This rate of success suggests that the juvenile liaison scheme should be extended to every police force: it is surprising that in the whole Metropolitan district, there are still only three J.L.O.s, all at West Ham. The United States police have been doing juvenile case-work since 1899. The Albemarle Report urged more experiments in youth work in this country, and the Ingleby Report commended the aims and achievements of the J.L.O. scheme, although it withheld a full blessing because of feeling that the work demanded trained social-workers. Some probation and child-care officers are understandably jealous of their territory, but both are at present badly overworked: probation officers, whose maximum case-load should be 40–50, are frequently each having to deal with over 100 cases. Many policemen, because of the respect in which they are held and because they are often able to share in the interests and language of every kind of person, have been highly successful in this work. The real need would seem to be for some elementary lectures in social science and also perhaps mental disorders to be included in the training of at least some, and preferably all, police officers (as they are in many continental and American forces). To those who regret the 'blurring of an image' it can be answered that it does nothing but good for a policeman to be seen as someone other than a bogey-man. It is particularly important that parents among delinquent parts of the community should view the police as allies rather than enemies: in West Ham, 38 per cent of the cases originated in requests directly from parents, and the effect on relations with the public generally in the area has been described as 'very good' by the Commissioner.

In a remarkable recent statement (which some reformers say has caused them distress because of the amount of wind it has removed from their sails), the Prison Officers' Association asked for a new and more constructive role for its members. It desires this for the sake of the morale of its members 'who join the service full of high ideals of doing something to help others', but at present 'soon become disillusioned and even bitter and cynical'.[1] Some police officers, particularly among the policewomen, are developing with the general rise in education a wider view of their function. An extension of their role should be welcome if it increases its value in human terms, instead of making it the repository of the unwanted jobs of society: it would improve the standard of recruits at the same time as the co-operation of the public and the interest and morale of the force.

Policemen have always been social workers in their dealings with juveniles and their co-operation with social agencies: what is now necessary is that they should be trained for these tasks. The police station could become a constructive centre in each community. In the future, the training of policemen should recognize that, because much of their work is concerned with all those people who, for various reasons, are not integrated into society, the police are in many ways the most important social service of all.

[1] In Israel the police and prison services are combined. Here it might be preferable eventually to merge the prison and probation services.

CHAPTER 2

Efficiency

Although they are not the only measures of good policing, the most usual indices of police efficiency are the 'number of indictable offences known to the police' as a measure of their preventive effect, and the 'percentage cleared up' as a guide to their detective success. (See following graphs.)

These figures must be treated with reserve. It is impossible to estimate how many crimes lie, like an iceberg, unknown to the police, because of for example relatives' or employers' discretion. One large firm in a single year dealt with 371 cases of staff larceny without reporting any of them to the police. The proportion of blackmail, incest, and shoplifting that is reported must be particularly low. People also may not report a crime because they fail to recognize it as such or else because they wish to avoid the publicity or the trouble of giving evidence as a witness.

In the other direction, the total may be exaggerated by 'thefts' of articles which are only mislaid or borrowed – sometimes in order to claim the insurance (though, if fraudently, each of these incidents would be a crime and so not disturb the total). A number of offences are committed or cleared up in a different year from that in which they came to light. Others, particularly acts done by juveniles, have only recently come to be regarded as crimes. Similarly, matrimonial assaults which may not have been re-

44

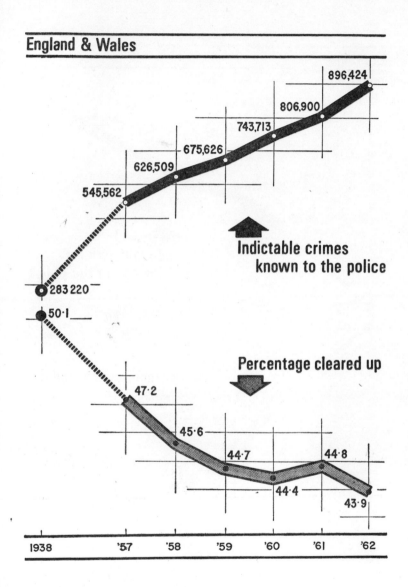

283 220

50·1

**Indictable crimes
known to the police**

545,562
626,509
675,626
743,713
806,900
896,424

Percentage cleared up

47·2
45·6
44·7
44·4
44·8
43·9

1938   '57   '58   '59   '60   '61   '62

45

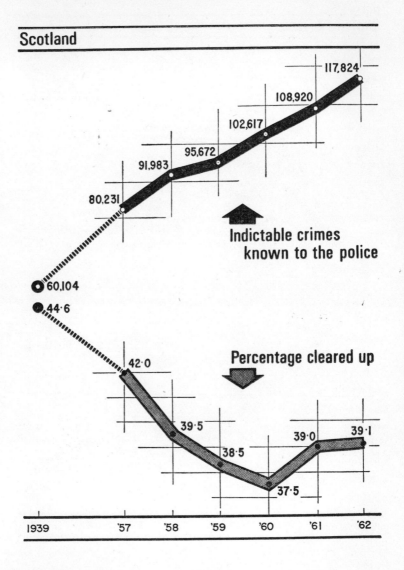

Scotland

117,824

108,920

102,617

95,672

91,983

80,231

Indictable crimes
known to the police

60,104
44·6

42·0

Percentage cleared up

39·5

38·5

39·0   39·1

37·5

1939   '57   '58   '59   '60   '61   '62

ported in slum areas may now be when the same community moves to a new housing estate.

Different police forces vary considerably in their policies and methods of classification, as well as in the amount of regard they pay to statistics. Some may wish to emphasize the seriousness of their crime situation in order to wring an increased budget or establishment from their local authority; others may be tempted to minimize the unsolved proportion by 'scrubbing' minor or insoluble offences, or the ones they feel belong to a neighbouring force.

Even when allowance is made for all these variables, the trend of both figures and their inter-relation disclose a serious situation. Despite the increase in education and prosperity, the number of serious crimes known to the police in England and Wales in 1960 was 262 per cent of the figure in 1938, while the population increased in that period only by a tenth. In Scotland the 1962 figure of 117,824 crimes is an increase of 43·2 per cent in ten years. The national position has sharply deteriorated even since the Royal Commission expressed 'concern'.

It is true that our crime situation is still not as serious as in the United States: Chicago and New York, for example, each have roughly double the annual number of murders we have in the whole of England and Wales, and only some 26 per cent of all serious American crimes are cleared up by arrest. But the fact that in this country the odds against detection are rising as well as the number of crimes has serious consequences. One is that police forces have increasingly been compelled to allot priorities in investigation. Understandably, offences against the person come first, both in importance and because they are more likely to be solved: 78 per cent of those in the Metropolitan area in 1962 were cleared up, compared with only 22 per cent of offences against property. Murder cases receive precedence: 170 were cleared up out of 175 in 1962. But urban C.I.D. officers candidly admit they have no time available for such things as attempting to trace stolen cars or car radios. Larceny of vehicles in London is so frequent that lists of over 1,000 become dead letters and the policeman on the beat can only remember a 'hot list' of the most recent thefts. The inevitable selection of laws and areas for enforcement causes irritation with householders and car-owners, who feel a need for the police only when they have personally lost something, and then discover their losses receive lowest priority of all. The 1962 clear-up rate in the Metropolitan area for housebreaking offences was only 15·6 per cent; for larcenies from vehicles in the street it was a bare 8·5 per cent. London, with its large shifting population and the lack of social cohesion characteristic of large cities, has always had the hardest crime problem of all (see the graph opposite).

Another serious consequence of the present situation is the likelihood that success in petty crime is acting as an encouragement to greater ambition. 'The belief is gaining hold in some quarters that crime pays,' reported the Inspectors of Constabulary in July 1960, and the increasing number of men who ask courts to take into consideration a list of undetected crimes sometimes running into three figures shows that the belief is making converts. No arrest has been made, nor has any of the money been recovered, in the case of the £¼ million stolen from the Post Office twelve years ago in the earliest of the recent highly organized robberies; the same is true of the even greater sum taken from Barclays Bank in four raids over the last three years. It seems that successful methods are being copied or else that successful gangs are growing bolder. Before the largest advertisement for crime of all, the Great Mail Train Robbery of August 1963, none of the earlier train robbers had been caught; and the same

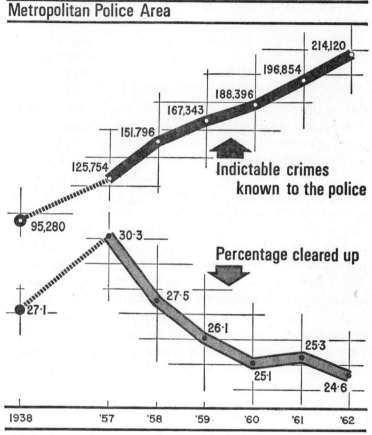

Metropolitan Police Area

214,120

196,854

188,396

167,343

151,796

125,754

Indictable crimes known to the police

95,280

30·3

Percentage cleared up

27·5

27·1

26·1

25·3

25·1

24·6

1938   '57   '58   '59   '60   '61   '62

trick of stopping a train by a red light had previously been used at Horsham. Whether it be cause or effect, more graduates must now be becoming criminals than policemen each year.

Casualties from road accidents as well have shown a sharp increase in the same period: from 208,000 in 1952 to 342,000 in 1962. The number of motor vehicles which the police have to control has doubled in the last ten years. The Metropolitan Commissioner told the Royal Commission:

> In the last twenty years complaints of crime have increased increased by 70 per cent; summonses issued by over 66 per cent; persons arrested and dealt with by the courts by 70 per cent; and vehicle accidents reported by over 90 per cent.

But at this time of growth in crime, traffic, and duties, some police forces are still seriously below strength, and the authorized establishments underestimate the real needs. Compared with New York City's 24,600, the Metropolitan Police at the beginning of 1963 had a strength of 17,776 – which is less than the 18,511 they had in 1938. Their authorized strength is 20,160, but the Commissioner has estimated that 25,000 would be a more realistic figure. Twenty-one police stations in the Metropolitan Area are at present closed down during the night. The respite gained by the reform of the law on street betting and prostitution has been swallowed up; meanwhile fresh problems have arisen in new techniques of political demonstration, and the racial tension while the latest wave of immigrants is being assimilated into our mongrel nation. As the urban spread continues, some areas can be covered only by motor patrols, and in others one constable is trying to man two or more beats. The Royal Commission visited one town with a population of 110,000 where only three men were on the beat, and these were all probationers. There is some correlation between the strength of the police and the discouragement of crime in both boroughs and counties: Sunderland with 144 policemen per 100,000 population has a clear-up rate of 49·5 per cent, whereas Leicester with 163 has one of 50·7 per cent, and Dewsbury with 170 one of 53·7 per cent. Similarly Wiltshire with a strength per 100,000 people of 120 has a clear-up rate of 46·7 per cent, while Lancashire with 143 has one of 48·6 per cent, and Cambridgeshire with 156 one of 53·8 per cent. Leeds, the Chairman of whose Watch Committee informed the Royal Commission that they had found it possible to reduce their police force, had to increase the police working week in 1963 from 44 to 48 hours because crime had quadrupled in the last seven years.

The rapid increase recently in the various private security companies is one symptom of the gaps left by the police through our keeping them short of men and equipment: Securicor, for example, which had fewer than 1,000 men two years ago, now employs 3,200. There are reports in other areas of citizens forming their own vigilantes' patrols against vandals. In addition insurance companies, who employ their own detectives on claims of over £150, are able to increase their rewards and sometimes pay their own informers more than the police because they have more money at their disposal. It was surprising that when the Government in 1963 ordered urgent investigations none of the 'Spies for Peace' was caught. More recently, administrative failures in the Woolf and Gordon cases gave rise to rumours that damaged the police. The harm that such mistakes can cause was shown by the earlier error which allowed the murderer Christie to be enrolled as a Reserve policeman despite his nine previous convictions ranging from fraud to violence.

The pattern and quality of crimes have changed since

51

the coming of the motor-car, and they are likely to become increasingly organized in a future of motorways and aircraft. Some criminal leaders are now known to look after the families of men who are caught, or to plan a jail-break in order to obtain a specialist for a particular job. Thieves, frequently living in one police area and operating in another, have been reported driving up to houses with removal vans and gutting them of furniture. One detective-superintendent spoke with admiration of the training which enables gangs today to back a lorry into a warehouse yard, break in, load, and drive off within five minutes.

The root of the problem of overwork in the police lies in the C.I.D., where some men are working more than 70 hours a week and cannot do more without risk of breaking down from the strain. The Dixon Committee said that the most any one detective can handle properly is 150 cases a year: but case-loads in London at present range from 150 to 564, with an average of 284 compared with 258 in 1958 and 205 in 1938. Each detective in 'F' division at Paddington is trying to cope with over 400 cases a year. Although there is a wide variation in the amount of work an individual case requires – a fraud investigation like the de Courcey case occupied two men for thirty months – even a motoring summons may consume sixteen hours of paperwork alone. Sir Ronald Howe said that if a detective has more than one case to work on in a week it is too much for him to do properly; in 1963 Edgar Hoover described a case-load of 20 per F.B.I. agent as 'too high' to a Congressional Sub-Committee. Whereas Maigret and his team on television often have a fortnight to deal with a single crime, in Leeds for example last year six detectives had to investigate 100 cases in that time. C.I.D. officers are paid for only three hours' overtime a week irrespective of how much they do, but in the Metropolitan Area at present the lower ranks are working an average of 13 extra hours and the senior ones 17 hours or more each week, even before the basic working week is reduced in July 1964. The best Scotland Yard officers are frequently away on loan; when Plymouth sent a request for a member of the Murder Squad in November 1963, there was no one available to go. On each occasion that an experienced detective officer retires or is moved, invaluable information is lost, and detectives complain that at present they simply have not the time to cultivate contacts and gather fresh information.

If the trend of crime is to be reversed, the number of C.I.D. officers needs to be doubled. There has always been a waiting list of men wishing to transfer to the C.I.D. – chiefly because of its greater independence. But a chief constable who increases the proportion of detectives in his force by transferring uniformed men from the beat risks starting a vicious circle with an increased number of crimes to be solved.

The situation is no criticism of the police or the Home Office, but rather of the public and local Police Authorities who deprive them of the men and equipment needed for modern conditions. In 1962 we spent about £130 million on 87,432 police employees in England and Wales, whereas the F.B.I. in America are spending in 1964 $147 million on only 14,000 employees. We should, for example, employ some professional accountants to help the Fraud Squad: several prosecutions have not been launched until after detailed exposures had been made by newspapers despite the risk of libel. As our national wealth has multiplied, we have failed to make any corresponding expansion in the means of protecting the increased amount of property. The total being spent at present in this country on experiments in crime prevention is less than £50,000 per annum, whereas in the United States the current budget on one such project alone is $12·5 million.

The C.I.D. all over the country would like more modern equipment – 'not just the miserable old black car everybody knows'; detectives in some areas are having to use their own cars and even bicycles because they are so short of transport. The advantage they used to possess in having wireless has disappeared now that not only do criminals tune in on V.H.F. (sometimes transmitting false messages), but the press as well have powerful receivers, so that when a house in Hampstead was burgled recently five reporters were able to arrive twenty minutes before the police. The secretarial facilities for detectives can only be described as archaic: it is not uncommon for eleven sergeants and five inspectors to be waiting for the one ancient typewriter they have to share. There are only about 150 tape-recorders between all the Metropolitan police: some officers say that at least 1,000 could be usefully employed. The situation is the same elsewhere: the Chairman of the Scottish Police Federation told the Minister of State for Scotland in May 1963: 'We are concerned about the condition of police buildings and equipment. These leave a great deal to be desired. There is evidence of false economy and of neglect which can only impair efficiency.' Only 39 of the 176 police stations in the Metropolitan Area were built since 1910. New Scotland Yard, constructed in 1890 with Dartmoor granite on foundations intended for an opera-house, is overflowing and badly in need of rebuilding.

The forensic laboratories are under such pressure that

they are able to concentrate on only the most serious cases and have no time to do any research except on an *ad hoc* basis. They are understaffed because scientists prefer to work elsewhere at higher salaries rather than to spend their time waiting at and being attacked in courts. Doctors are for the same reason frequently reluctant to help the police, who sometimes have to contact twelve or more before finding one who is prepared to come and examine a drunk motorist: the Nottingham force estimates that 70 per cent of drivers who are drunk when arrested are able to sober up before a doctor can be found to test them.

Improvements in the police will require more money, but the expense will always be a small fraction of the cost of the crime. Each prison sentence costs the community an average of £2,500. Hoover estimates the United States' annual crime bill to be $22 billion. The Metropolitan Police in 1962 had records of over £12 million being stolen, of which less than £2½ million was recovered. The cost of road accidents in Britain in 1962 was estimated by the Royal Society for the Prevention of Accidents to be £227 million. But the real damage that crime and road casualties cause, in human terms, is incalculable.

What can be done to make our police more efficient? Any appreciable increase in manpower is unlikely in present conditions. The ratio of population per policeman has, in fact, already been steadily decreasing:

Annual Number of Population per Police Officer in England and Wales

1952 : 611	1956 : 602	1960 : 594
1953 : 610	1957 : 598	1961 : 590
1954 : 607	1958 : 598	1962 : 581
1955 : 606	1959 : 598	

Scotland 1962 : 539

55

But by comparison, the figure in the U.S.A. is 502, in Western Germany 391, and in France 329. Furthermore at the end of 1962 only 6 forces out of the 125 in England and Wales and 6 out of the 33 in Scotland were at their full strength. Chief constables say it is the way of life and conditions of work which are responsible for the vacancies, and that these, unlike pay, cannot be altered. 'The main disadvantage of police lie anywhere,' said Sir Joseph Simpson, the Metropolitan Commissioner, in July 1963, 'is the necessity for duty to cover the whole of the twenty-four hours a day, seven days a week, in contrast to the bulk of the population whose working day is over by 6 p.m.' Nor, chief constables say, are they able to lower standards of recruitment any further. Too often, however, by 'standard' they are thinking of some physical measurement: the City of London force, for example, which is 22 per cent below strength still insists on a minimum height of 5 ft 11 in., while 5 ft 8 in. suffices for the rest of London. Many administrative and detective posts in the police might surely be filled by men who fall short of the mandatory requirements of chest measurement.

Traffic wardens cost only £17 per week each compared with £30 for a police constable, and they are also easier to recruit because they are not subject to such strict requirements of physique and age. At present they deal only with stationary vehicles. Their work could easily be expanded to control zebra crossings (civilians already successfully operate school crossings), and they could also undertake general traffic duties at the peak hours, when at present police officers have to be brought in off the beat twice a day. In addition, this policy would increase the interest of the wardens' role – its present negative and limited nature is responsible for a high rate of early resignations. (It is interesting that in Algeria since Independence boy Scouts have been doing traffic duty on one day a week when the regular policeman has his rest-day. They even have powers to arrest and fine. The system is reported to work well and solves the problem caused by the withdrawal of the French police.)

Powers to give a ticket and to impose a fine on the spot when a motorist admits an offence would save hundreds of policemen-hours in court each day. The simplification of traffic regulations would benefit both police and motorists. The absence of a standard rule for priority at roundabouts and many cross-roads not only causes accidents but wastes police time on duty at them.

Leicester has made a successful experiment in employing female traffic wardens: there are reports that their politeness causes less resentment from irate motorists. Policewomen in general are good for contact with the public at points of irritation: only 14 out of the 1722 complaints in the Metropolitan area in 1962 were against female officers. The proportion of women in the force could profitably be raised from the present 3 per cent to 5 per cent. Their role is at the moment unnecessarily constricted by male prejudice. They have been allowed a vote only in the past two years by the Police Federation (who told the Bridgeman Committee – without adducing any evidence: 'The very nature of the duties of a P.C. are contrary to that which is finest and best in woman').

There is room as well for many more civilian clerical staff, who are not so difficult to recruit as uniformed men and women. They are also more economical because they do not need to qualify for the exceptionally early pension which is awarded to policemen after 25 years' service. They could save trained detectives the valuable time they spend typing their reports with one finger. Bradford after the war attached two shorthand-typists to each division to act as secretaries to the C.I.D. As a result, the time the detectives were able to spend in the actual investigation of crimes increased from 55 per cent to 85 per cent, and the clear-up rate rose accordingly. Despite the Oaksey Committee's recommendation that this should be followed everywhere, it has not yet been done. One police officer said: 'When I joined this force it was 196 strong and now it is about 350, yet there are no extra men out on the beat. All these additional men have been swallowed up by paperwork and the specialist departments. That's the chief problem with the job now: you're tied down with paperwork when you should be out on the beat.' For a single traffic case, it may be necessary for the officer concerned to write a report in the accident book, seek statements, and then type them out with his own comments and summary. He must then prepare copies of plans and photographs, organize medical or forensic evidence, and check records (criminal, employers', and Service) besides the insurance and car and driving licences. Finally, he may have to prepare the brief for the Prosecution – as well as serve the summons, call on and notify witnesses, and perhaps liaise with another police force if the defendant is not a local man.

The Criminal Justice Act 1948 and subsequent measures have resulted in a great increase in the amount of police written reports. There is a strong case for much new office equipment being provided immediately for them. Business efficiency experts should be called in by every force to advise how paperwork might be reduced by, for example, greater use of pro-formae and tape-recorders. Many magistrates' courts would also save hours if depositions were no longer laboriously written out in longhand. The general streamlining of committal proceedings might make members of the public less reluctant to give evidence, as well as save the police time spent on matters which are often not in dispute at all.

We should make a radical cost-analysis of the employment of police manpower on, for example, traffic duties, along the same lines that Dennis Healey advocates should be done for our foreign policies. From July 1964 the present 44-hour working week of a policeman will be reduced to one of 42 hours. If the police were relieved ot some of their unnecessary functions, it would be possible to improve recruiting by introducing a week of 40 hours. Eleven years after the Burrell Committee on Police Extraneous Duties reported that the police should not perform them, at least 11 forces are still changing street parking signs, 8 collect the money due under maintenance orders, and in 8 men are serving as civic mace bearers. Many policemen are still to be seen every day acting as ushers in courts. In 11 forces policemen do duty as mortuary attendants, and in others they act as market inspectors. Some are still required to keep domestic servants' registers, and to license and inspect hackney carriages. Others are also performing the duties the Burrell Committee reported that they should not under the Shops Act 1950, Weights and Measures Acts, Petroleum Acts, and Pharmacy and Poisons Acts.

West Sussex and Cornwall, among others, have recently made organizations and methods studies. The chairman of the latter's Police Authority in January 1964 described their survey's report as 'very far-reaching and in some respects alarming'. The findings should be put to national and not just local use. This fragmentation of research and of the capital necessary for it has been a recurrent handicap for our police forces. In the words of one chief constable, 'economy and not efficiency has been the overriding influence in the persuasion of each local authority'. The result has been duplication of research by forces unaware of what is going on elsewhere.

Co-ordination of the enterprise of individual forces will be one of the tasks of the new Research and Planning Branch set up at the Home Office under the Chief Inspector of Constabulary, Sir Edward Dodd. The budget for its first year – £43,000 – is minute compared to the amount spent each week on the research programme for the armed forces. There is no reason why such a body should not have been set up decades ago: it did not require statutory enactment, and its purpose of giving 'top priority to the problems of grave and unsolved crimes' is no novel necessity. For too long Home Secretaries, despite their residual responsibility for law and order, sheltered behind the phrase 'no responsibility without any power'. There was no reason other than apathy why a Chief Inspector of Constabulary should have been appointed years before 1963. Successive Home Secretaries told Parliament there was no need for more Inspectors, although they have always possessed the power to increase their number as was recommended by the Royal Commission. Nineteen other recommendations were able to be implemented without waiting for the Police Bill. Hitherto the visits of inspection of forces have been so brief and so well advertised in advance that it is not surprising that Brighton was certified as efficient between 1951 and 1958, or Worcester in 1957 (the year before the then chief constable was sentenced to 18 months' imprisonment for the fraudulent conversion of police funds). One police officer said that 'by the time the band had played at the parade, buttons had been inspected, the most promising recruit had had his hand shaken, and the papers laid out on top appreciated, the visit was over'. In future inspections will last for a full week, instead of the day or two hitherto, and the Inspectors have each been provided with a staff officer and a shorthand-writer. But it is unfortunate that the Metropolitan force – easily the largest and a quarter of the country's total strength – will still not be inspected. This is a grave omission when knowledge about the progress made by other forces still depends largely on its dissemination by the Inspectors. Many people also regret that the Inspectorate does not include, for instance, a senior civil servant who could watch administrative efficiency, an accountant who might advise on economy, an educationalist to discuss training, or a lawyer who could look at complaints.

Inspectors will still have the power only to suggest improvements or standardizations to chief constables. There is plenty of scope: within sixty minutes a criminal in the Manchester area would be able to cross six police areas, each of which operates on a different wireless frequency. Police forces' networks should not only be co-ordinated, but should also be coded: Southampton has successfully introduced such a code (with a card index in patrol cars), but messages in the Metropolitan area are still being interrupted, sometimes by taxi-drivers in France.

Some pocket transistor sets are supplied to men on the beat in Lancashire and are popular – the solitary constable feels less isolated when he is able to ask for help or advice at any time. They are also frequently able to reduce the fatal time-lag before the police get to the scene of a crime, at present due to the man on the beat being out of contact although he may be quite near. Their eventual adoption everywhere seems inevitable. One chief constable considers that the Treasury should authorize 20,000 two-way portable sets immediately, despite their cost of £135 each ('further research' often really means 'further economies'); he estimates that a policeman on the beat who has one can do the work of one and a half men without. Since one policeman costs £1,500 a year, the outlay of their cost would soon be recouped.

Although the New York police possess several helicopters, Durham is the only force in this country at present which even has one on hire, apart from an experimental one on the M.6. Experience has shown their value in traffic control, especially on the motorways where cars cannot turn round, and also for aerial photography and searching. When provided with a direct wireless link to patrol cars, they can also be used for crime prevention as an 'eye-in-the-sky' on the movement of valuable consignments. Here is one field for the supporters of the present fragmentation to show that co-operation between forces is as satisfactory as they allege, for it is well known that several other chief constables would like helicopters but that their local authorities have not felt able to afford one. A unified force could be equipped with a helicopter or a light plane in each region of the country.

The most serious deficiency of all is the fact that, although more than 84 different police forces in the United States are using computers or data-processing equipment, not one force in England, Wales, or Scotland yet has access to one. They would lead to an enormous saving of police work in administration, records, and statistics, and could revolutionize the field of detection by the elimination of suspects. One force in America, for example, Dade County in Florida, makes use of its equipment in the following ways:

(1) Data-processing all accident reports, so that a computer can help prepare quick analyses of causes and black-spots, which enables accident-prevention measures to be taken daily and the information to be made available to the public, insurance companies, lawyers, etc.

(2) Classifying crimes rapidly according to characteristics, locality, etc. by means of a punched-card system.

(3) Rapid indentification of fingerprints by a data-processing programme which can cope even with incomplete prints.

(4) Data-processing and retyping to other forces details of arrests every 24 hours.

(5) Every month, a complete operational time analysis is made of all cases, calls, and communications, from which the Planning Division can draw up a 'comprehensive selective enforcement and prevention campaign'.

(6) Recording all stolen and recovered property by statistical data-processing.

At present one print may take 10 of the 134 men employed at the Fingerprint Department at Scotland Yard six weeks' searching to find, whereas the New York computer can compare 100,000 fingerprints in three hours. Modern equipment would also benefit the 'Method of Crime' Departments, which play a highly important role because the majority of criminals are specialists and rarely change their techniques. In the future forces should be able to exchange fingerprints, photographs, and records by phototelegraphy. Unfortunately at present the Criminal Record Offices here do not even cover the whole country because, the Royal Commission found, 'individual chief constables prefer to remain outside the district organization'. Nor does the National Record Office at Scotland Yard always send to local forces the fingerprints of criminals known to be in their area. The Home Office has plans at the moment for a computer which could handle police pay, thereby resulting in a saving of some 200 clerks in this department. Obviously here could be the lead for the research into other uses, followed by the provision of perhaps regional computers if they are too expensive for individual forces.

In the past the police, rightly recognizing the value of experience, local knowledge, and common sense, have not always taken easily to science. Fingerprinting had been used in India for a hundred years before it replaced Scotland Yard's methods of anatomical measurement following the terrible miscarriage of justice in the case of Beck, who was wrongly identified by twelve witnesses (and whose years in prison also contributed to the establishment of the Court of Criminal Appeal). For the new equipment to be effective, it will be necessary to train each individual police officer to think in scientific terms. Fortunately the Police Federation recognize they have nothing to fear from such developments, and indeed would even welcome them. One day we hope that Britain will join other countries in sending many policemen on university courses. They could study, for example, traffic planning, to gain a constructive approach to an unpopular part of their duty, while at the same time contributing their own experience.

The chief constable of Durham, Mr Alec Muir, has pioneered the way in creating a scientific climate by producing since 1959 a quarterly *Which?*-type bulletin evaluating new police equipment. Lancashire has also been a leader under its vigorous chief constable, Col. T.

E. Johnston, developing the pocket transmitter entirely in the county police's own workshops. Lancashire was the first force in Britain to employ radar in 1957 – although it had already been used for ten years by the American police and for three by the Canadians. In the same way as fingerprint evidence almost inevitably ensures a conviction, the maximum use of scientific equipment like radar and breathalysers would reduce the area of attack on the police in courts – to the benefit of everyone except the guilty. The possibility might also be investigated of filming drunk motorists. The Swiss traffic police save much dispute by providing drivers with immediate photographs of traffic offences, which show the speed meter reading and the number plate of the vehicle. Much more research remains to be done in methods of photography and security (at present over 97 per cent of burglar-alarm calls are false alarms, generally due to bad maintenance), and in the use of infra-red spectro-photometry, television, and tape-recorded evidence. A machine has been developed which, while a man writes, records the message at headquarters: this would be invaluable for speeding reports, when a few minutes so often make all the difference between a crime being 'cleared up' and merely 'known to the police'.

'The speedy transmission of valuable information is the basis of all criminal investigation,' said Sir Richard Jackson, as one of his reasons for arousing British interest in Interpol whose importance has grown as crime becomes increasingly international and the speed of transport develops. (It has a rigorous rule to concern itself only with crimes that are universally recognized, and not those that are political, racial, or religious: South Africa and Eastern Europe have consequently withdrawn, and in 1959 the Annual Conference was cancelled because the host country refused to issue visas for Israeli delegates.) There should be much more international exchange of methods and experience of crime prevention and treatment: often many individual countries are laboriously seeking the same solutions, in the same way that scores of individual police forces in Britain are making identical elementary experiments. For example, a photographic technique had been evolved in Italy by which even the thickness of paint can be measured. Other continental forces have developed methods of controlling traffic by closed-circuit television, which is linked to traffic lights that adjust 800 times a day with changes in the flow, and has been shown to save motorists up to twenty minutes per rush hour. New York has perfected a three-dimensional form of the Identi-Kit – the somewhat crude aid to identification which caught public imagination by helping to solve a murder within the first week of its introduction in Britain in 1961, after it had been demonstrated to Jackson by the Sheriff of Los Angeles County.

Apart from rationalizations in manpower and equipment, the greatest help, in the view of the police themselves, would be to simplify and eventually to codify our laws. Reforms of this nature may well have to await a new government department devoted to justice, with academics and laymen as well as lawyers giving a sustained hard stare at our legal system. But ultimately it will always remain the ordinary member of the public who is really responsible for the degree of police success: it depends more than any other factor on his co-operation and recognition of his responsibility for crime prevention. One day we will also recognize the wisdom of giving equipment to the police which is superior to that of the criminals.

CHAPTER 3

Freedom from Crime

The work of the police could undoubtedly also be made much easier if a re-examination was made of their legal powers. We have always thought it preferable to keep these too small rather than have them too great. John Stuart Mill commented: 'In England there has always been more liberty, but worse organization, while in other countries there is better organization but less liberty.' But there is a less understandable pride in this country in keeping the boundaries of these powers uncertain and un-written: between what the police may, and may not do, there is a non-man's-land which is still disputed in the courts. It is time that this uncertainty was cleared up. At present, policemen complain that their work has become more difficult because members of the public are increasingly aware of their rights. In the past the police have been used to relying largely on bluff when, for example, inviting someone to give his name or to come with them for questioning. It is equally anomalous that their powers at present vary in different parts of England: the police may stop, search, and detain someone on suspicion in London, Manchester, Birmingham, Hertford, Blackburn, Rochdale, Birkenhead, Salford, Liverpool, Chester, Wallasey, Wolverhampton, Barrow-in-Furness, Southend, Rotherham, and Southampton, but not anywhere else. One very senior police officer said: 'There's nothing wrong with the law as it is, you can always get round it.' It would be a healthier situation if the police were given whatever clearly defined powers are considered necessary for them to do their work, and then never permitted to exceed their limits.

At least then the solution to the paradox of social values described in Chapter One could be clearly judged. This chapter examines a number of points at which the needs of civil liberty and prevention of crime meet and conflict. How we resolve the conflict depends on how highly we prize each relative need. It is important to realize that each area is controversial only because it does involve deep-rooted social values. Indeed the police make a fascinating study precisely because almost everything they do reflects the social and personal tenets by which we live. This is seen in turn in questions of identification, search, detention for questioning, privacy, allegations against police witnesses, presumption of innocence, the new Judges' Rules, 'Fifth Amendment' pleading, and voluntary statements. The reader will resolve each matter in the light of his own social and personal criteria.

Which are the powers the police should possess is a matter of the highest importance, and one that arouses correspondingly strong feelings. It is all the more necessary that the subject should be studied with a rational approach, and that emotional words such as 'un-English' – employed with equal facility and lack of definition by anarchists and authoritarians alike – should be avoided. The onus of justification should be on those who suggest that the police *should* possess any particular power. The criteria by which each power should be tested are: (1) will it jeopardize any innocent man? and (2) if not, will it increase our freedom from crime? Jeremy Bentham, who believed that the object of any law should be to augment the total happiness of the community, was in favour of police for preventing and ensuring the punishment of crimes, but stipulated that 'no method of prevention should be employed which is likely to cause a greater mischief than the offence itself'. He said that police were 'destined to prevent evils and provide benefits', but only on condition that their powers were clearly laid down. In this, as in some of his other suggestions – for full legal aid, compensation for victims of crimes of violence, and for people carrying identity marks – he was in advance of our present development.

Penal reformers, from Bentham and Romilly down to Lord Gardiner, have advocated that the cure for crime lies in making its punishment more certain rather than more severe. (Probably the only influence which deterrent sentences have is in inverse proportion to the gravity of the offence: they may have some effect on, for example, motoring offenders.) Research shows that 85 per cent of first offenders who are caught are not recorded as offending again; this is not only the highest, but virtually the only clearly established factor that is known to discourage crime. Certainty of detection is a *sine qua non* whatever views are held as to the subsequent treatment of the criminal. Peel's belief in 1829 that a larger and better-equipped police force would result in and is a necessary prerequisite for penal reform is equally true today.

Even if people believe that the British system in any field is the best in the world, it should still be kept under continual dispassionate examination and improved. Some people have recently said that the incessant advance of crime is a sign that the police's powers of investigation are inadequate. It is, however, essential that our approach to the problem is activated not by any short-term pressure but by as scientific as possible an assessment of what is best for the community.

Certain of the powers of the police at present may be thought too wide, or too vague: other additions might possibly be made which could not conceivably prejudice any innocent person. It is difficult to see who, except someone who has just committed a crime, could reasonably object to telling a police officer his name and address; yet the police at present are frequently handicapped by having no power to discover these elementary facts. For instance, a policeman who sees some people committing misdemeanours is often helpless because he is neither able to order them to wait so that he can charge them, nor does he have any means of discovering who they are. Rapid identification would operate to the benefit of innocent people by enabling suspects to be eliminated quickly. In many Commonwealth countries the police have the right to take into custody anyone who refuses to give his name and address: police officers here think that this is reasonable 'for it is just the criminal types who are awkward and the ones you want to be able to trace'. If everybody carried an identity card as they did in war-time, it would be possible to name not only bodies, but also people found suffering from loss of memory, who sometimes at present have to be kept unnecessarily in hospital for weeks. Such a card could save lives if it recorded the blood-group of the owner. It is essential to know the correct name – and hence the history – of a man, in order to be able to give him the appropriate treatment, whether medical (including mental) or penal.

In addition, the likelihood of being asked to prove one's identity would discourage cheque-frauds and other forgeries. In order to obviate the possibility of false papers, in some parts of India it is necessary to give one's fingerprint before cashing a cheque. Fingerprints are the one totally infallible means of identification. No two fingers or toes are ever identical, even belonging to the same person or otherwise identical twins. Neither do the characteristics of the ridges of their skin ever change: if a person loses this skin, the ridges regrow exactly the same. The prints are in fact the marks formed by a thin coating of grease which covers every finger, and they have been identified on clothing and even through gloves. At present in this country, if a man is acquitted his fingerprints are burnt in the 'confidential waste sack' – even if the police are certain of his guilt and even if he gave his fingerprints voluntarily – despite there being no statutory obligation to destroy them. It is hard to see what any law-abiding person has to fear if his prints are kept in a permanent record. Because they are the most scientific, they are therefore the most impartial form of evidence possible. If everybody had their prints taken at an early age (they are clearly formed before birth), the idea of that being any more degrading than being photographed would disappear; if they were filed for computers as was suggested in the previous chapter, they would be the greatest possible deterrent to crime throughout a person's life. Larceny, housebreaking, and receiving, the crimes in which prints are most commonly found, normally make up more than 80 per cent of all indictable offences – and are just those crimes which the police are now least able to clear up.

It is difficult to see how the duty to be correctly identified can be described as an infringement of civil liberty. Rather it is the opposite, for the correct scientific identification of the real culprit may avert a miscarriage of justice. There is a similar case to be made for a court to be able to order tests of saliva, semen, or blood, for their results might all contribute towards the establishment of innocence. If there were 'night courts', as there are in America, which could see drivers immediately and order a medical examination, a great deal of dispute would be saved. The more indisputable evidence there can be before a court, the greater possibility there is of justice being done.

The right to remain anonymous or wrongly identified is defended with a passion which is exceeded only by an Englishman's feelings about his home. Although other officials (such as gas and electricity inspectors) may do so, by law the police are not allowed to enter private premises, or to search them for stolen property or evidence, without an invitation from the owner (improbable in cases of guilt) or a warrant issued by a magistrate in the case of certain offences.

The 1929 Royal Commission stated that 'it had long been the practice of the police' to search arrested people's homes without any warrant, and that this 'is, in the main, necessary and proper in the interests of justice and cannot be regarded as in any way an undue infringement of the rights and liberties of the subject'; yet despite their recommendation that this should be 'regularized by statute' it still is not legal. Most policemen will frankly admit that it continues to happen frequently. In 1954 the police agreed that they searched both Mr Pitt-Rivers' and Lord Montagu's houses without either warrants or permission, but other courts have awarded damages for trespass against policemen who have done this.

The Commission's other unanimous recommendations for regularizing the position regarding 'detention for questioning' have also not yet been acted upon. The result is that the police again have to continue to resort to methods such as bluff or 'holding charges'. In one case in December 1958, a suspect was held for more than 80 hours at Holloway Police Station. Mr Claud Mullins, an experienced Stipendiary Magistrate, has said: 'At present, our police have no strict legal right to detain people for questioning in police stations, but they do and they need to do so. They could not conduct their investigations without this procedure. But its legality is questionable. Our police are under the necessity to take risks at times by going beyond the Judges' Rules. Because of hampering limitations the police are forced to act in ways that are not strictly legal. This gives rise to many misunderstandings between police and public.' The Willink Commission declined to deal with this subject, although several witnesses spoke of the effect it had on relations with the public.

Police officers themselves agree that if they were given adequate legal powers they would not have the excuse of frustration for resorting to extra-legal ones. Several policemen, discussing the new Judges' Rules, said that they had been revised 'because there is a general impression that we gild the lily'. They declared that: 'If we fully observed the Rules, new or old, we would be tying one hand behind our backs, and the public would be the first to howl at us because we never convicted anybody.' An experienced inspector commented, 'A good policeman remembers the Rules – when he is in the witness-box.'

Speed of search is essential if stolen property or vital evidence is to be recovered; but the difficulties under which the police at present labour is illustrated by their experience that if they guard a house while obtaining a search warrant they are laying themselves open to an action for defamation. One detective-superintendent at Scotland Yard said that he did not often apply for a warrant 'because the publicity it attracted was fatal'. With so little stolen property being recovered at the present time, thirty-five years would seem long enough to wait for the Royal Commission's recommendation to be implemented – especially if it was coupled with a provision for speedy compensation for any damage caused.

Certainly the situation should be regularized one way or the other: the present disbelief in many cases of the police's evidence that 'permission was obtained' does no good. It also leads to inconsistency in our law, because our courts allow tangible evidence including documents, but not confessions, to be admitted at a trial even if it has been illegally obtained. In the United States, the Supreme Court has since 1914 enforced in criminal (but not civil) cases the 'Tainted Evidence' rule whereby any evidence, however trustworthy or relevant, is inadmissible if it is 'tainted' by being obtained 'unreasonably'. It might be preferable to do the same here, but we would first of all have to give our police more adequate powers that are legal. At present they labour under considerable difficulties when they try to obtain evidence even outside private houses to bring offenders to justice. In a case in October 1963, the Court of Criminal Appeal ruled that two constables had no right to attempt to stop a car which they had reasonable grounds for believing would reveal evidence in a case of dangerous driving. As the law stands at the moment, they equally have no legitimate means of obtaining papers in a case of fraud or a weapon believed to have been used for murder – yet delay allows an intelligent criminal to alter the evidence so that it is lost for ever.

Privacy is a desirable quality, and it is especially valuable in modern life, but the community should decide how much of it is as important as justice.

It will always be vital, however, that people have confidence, as they do at the moment, that any information or evidence obtained by the police shall never be communicated to anyone else, whether member of the public, employer, or government department. Telephone-tapping is an illustration of the whole problem. The police are allowed, if they can show a cast-iron *prima facie* case of a very serious crime, to intercept telephone calls. In 1957 a Committee of Lord Birkett, Lord Monckton, and Mr Patrick Gordon-Walker examined the present practice and approved it. They were unanimous in declaring that 'so far from the citizen being injured by the exercise of the power in the circumstances we have set out, we think the citizen benefits therefrom'. Its value is demonstrated by the fact that in 1957 every interception but one led to arrest. The present position is, however, a compromise: the personal approval of the Home Secretary has to be obtained for each individual case, so that the power is used very rarely – about 50 times a year by the police in England and for several years in Scotland not at all. Many people believe that a Judge would be a more appropriate person than a politician to give such permission. If we accept the Committee's recommendation that 'the criminal and the wrong-doer should not be allowed to use services provided by the State for wrongful purposes quite unimpeded, and the police, the customs, and the security services ought not to be deprived of an effective weapon in their efforts to preserve and maintain order for the benefit of the community', it is difficult to see why such a weapon should be used so little. It is permitted with varying safeguards elsewhere: for example, in the United States, Italy, Austria, Scandinavia, Switzerland, Germany, and France. It is possible to argue that no innocent person need worry if his telephone is being tapped, and that wider use of this power could prevent many cases of business fraud and blackmail – two of the hardest crimes to prove before great damage has been caused. But if the police are to have this power at all, it is essential that the information obtained is never passed to any outside body, such as the Birkett Committee criticized Lord Tenby for having permitted when he was Home Secretary. Fortunately in this country tapping by private people is virtually impossible, for technical reasons – unlike in America, where it is used by commercial rivals. Whether an intercepted conversation should be admitted as evidence at a trial is a separate question, which presumably depends on proof that the method of recording was reliable and that the entire conversation is before the court.

In 1963 Holborn Borough Council turned down a recommendation of their Highways Committee that plain-clothes wardens should be employed to prevent meter-feeding, on the grounds that it would be 'distasteful' – although motorists who are unable to find an empty meter, and know that this feeding vitiates the whole scheme might not agree. But many people have a deep-seated feeling that the use of plain clothes or eavesdropping is 'unsporting', and this inhibits wider employment of them, even though their use is accepted where some crimes or the security of the state are involved. The C.I.D. were opposed for a long time in the last century on the grounds that they were 'snoopers'. This 'sporting' attitude stems from the days of revulsion against the earlier bar-

barity of the criminal law and its methods. But anybody who takes a romantic view of crime today should go to a criminal court and see its true human consequences – in the unhappiness, broken families, and the fear and suspicion it can arouse in people. It is to the benefit of everybody, the more justice can be made a science and the less a sport. Crime, and to be suspected of it, are both serious matters. A suspect is not a pheasant: he is entitled at his trial to something other than luck.

The main protections of the citizen against police oppression are his ability to apply to the courts for *habeas corpus* to stop wrongful imprisonment, and to sue a police officer who has exceeded his powers. The new Police Bill is to be welcomed for making the latter easier, by enabling chief constables to be sued for any of their force's illegal acts and providing that consequent damages or costs shall be paid out of the police fund. However, unless he has some corroboration, a complainant's word is rarely accepted against that of the police. A defendant in a criminal trial faces a further risk from our rule that any criminal history which he has is liable to be revealed in court if he makes an allegation against a police witness. This threat introduces a disagreeable element of gambling into a trial, and should be abolished. It is a fundamental part of justice that a man is tried for the matter he is accused of, and not for the smear of his previous history. The fact that a man has a criminal record should not deny him the right to speak of anything irregular that has happened to him – especially as almost all police misconduct takes place against known criminals. Neither does it necessarily follow that the word of such a man is worthless – some of the most criminal people are truthful, and some of the most law-abiding confirmed fantasists.

The other great bastion of civil rights on which we pride ourselves is the presumption of innocence. But this is reversed in some offences: under the Prevention of Crimes Act, 1871, whereby a man with a criminal past may be jailed for a year on suspicion, and in the Vagrancy Act, 1824, by which anyone, even without a previous bad character, can be imprisoned for suspiciously 'loitering', although 'it shall not be necessary to show that the prisoner was guilty of any particular act or acts tending to show his purpose or intent'. Previous convictions are given as evidence in these cases. It is possible to convict law-abiding people of the infamous charge of 'sus' for nothing more than looking in two shop-windows. An ex-chief inspector has said: 'This is a much abused provision, and one of tyrannical scope. . . . It has also given rise to many injustices, and many convictions on evidence falling far short of the standards required in other criminal cases.' It should be repealed immediately, and the police given powers instead to catch those who are actually guilty.

The most discussed and disputed actions of the police occur when they question suspects. In general they have no power to compel any witness or suspect either to disclose any fact within his knowledge or to answer any question. The conditions necessary before any statement or confession is admitted as evidence in a trial have lately been revised by the High Court Judges. These 'Judges' Rules' were first formulated in 1912, after two policemen had been censured by two different Judges, one for 'cautioning' and the other one for not doing so. The new Rules contain improvements for ensuring fairness and for giving the police more chances to question. They have been criticized for both, but probably their main defect is that they are so complicated that they are unlikely to be observed. But it is even more doubtful whether the 'caution', on which the old and new Rules are based, fulfils any useful purpose: does the well-worn formula really prevent any innocent person from making a false confession? In the absence of physical or mental pressure (in conjunction with which no 'caution' will make any difference) wrong confessions will only emanate either deliberately or, more commonly, from the mentally ill. On neither of these categories is the caution likely to have any effect. Not only is it a chimerical safeguard but, when it is scrupulously administered it must often cut off a valuable flood of information – relating perhaps to other crimes or the whereabouts of stolen property – which a guilty man is anxious to volunteer in explanation of his actions. Is it in the public interest that really voluntary and accurate confessions, or even the significance of false statements, are excluded from being evidence merely because of the absence of this formula? The real safeguards we need in order to be satisfied about a statement are (1) that it was made voluntarily, and (2) that it is reproduced in full. The present arrangements are unsatisfactory because they fail to meet fully either of these requirements.

One solution for ensuring them would be to allow questioning only when an impartial third person is present: whether he was a solicitor, shorthand-writer, or even a bystander, he would be able equally to verify fairness and to protect the police from unjust allegations. At present suspects who are poor sometimes receive less justice than rich people who can insist on their solicitors' presence. Some solicitors say they would be prepared to join a panel who could be summoned to be present during

79

questioning at any time. It would neither be necessary nor desirable to allow them to interrupt or advise silence: their mere presence would be enough to ensure fairness. In a case in 1950, the Court of Criminal Appeal approved notes taken by a shorthand-writer at an interrogation as being the fairest and best record. Alternatively, a tamper-proof form of tape-recording could reproduce the questions, together with the pauses and the tone of voice, although it might miss other factors only discernible to the eye. Locked cassettes or clock-mechanisms can make tape-recordings more reliable evidence than notebooks or even photographs. If it is objected that the full recording would be too long or incoherent for a jury to follow, the solution would be to make it all available to the defence, so that they could refer to any particular part if they wished.

The new Rules advise the police to allow everybody to write out their own statement (one Judge who was charged with a motoring offence recently insisted on doing so in the policeman's notebook). When the police do the writing, it becomes hearsay evidence by being translated into police language. If the revised Judges' Rules are thought to ensure fairness, their principles should be applied to the questioning of witnesses as well. But, as one Judge comments, 'They do not lay down what the police may or may not do at the police station to obtain information, provided it is proved in court by some other means.' The Home Office has issued some 'administrative directions' to all police forces regarding their methods of taking statements, though, like the Judges' Rules, these are not part of the law. (See Appendix).

Some recent cases have resulted in the suggestion that the police should have greater legal powers to ensure the presence of witnesses at court: by being, for example, able to extradite them. Extradition, whether or not extended to witnesses, should cover all except political offenders, instead of the present somewhat arbitary categories. The 'Spot' case showed the necessity for protecting witnesses, but it would be unjustifiable interference to take them into custody, as a few people advocate: in the United States, two unfortunate law-abiding sisters recently spent six months in gaol because they were unable to raise a large bond.

In most Continental countries, the *juge d'instruction* can examine people who are believed to have relevant information in addition to the suspect himself. In some jurisdictions these people can be penalized if they refuse to answer questions. This system has two major advantages over our own 'accusatorial' method. First, it is to society's advantage to learn as much as possible concerning the reasons for every crime – an aspect which often totally fails to emerge in English courts. Secondly, and of even greater importance, the more thorough the investigation of a crime, the less chance there is of a wrong conviction. For most people, however, the long delays of the European system are a disadvantage which outweighs the benefits; but there should be comparative research to discover if these delays are inescapable, and whether both systems might not profit by adopting parts of each other's procedure.

In English-speaking countries witnesses can be subpoenaed to appear in court, but they are under no obligation to answer any question that might incriminate them – often the questions to which their answers might be most valuable. By pleading the Fifth Amendment some men in America have been able to evade conviction for years. In both countries the person who is actually charged with a crime enjoys an even greater right: not only need he not answer, but he need not even be questioned in court if he does not so desire. This is the high-water mark of the 'sporting' attitude in the law. Support for the rule (which is not an ancient one) seems to have originated in reaction to the days of torture, when suspects were almost invariably uneducated men facing the death penalty. It has been widely criticized since. The American National Commission on Law Observance in 1931 stated that they considered that this privilege 'has come to be of little advantage to the innocent and a mere piece in the game of criminal justice'. Bentham described the rule as 'one of the most pernicious and most irrational notions that ever found its way into the human mind', and went on:

> If it is wished to protect the accused against punishment, it can be done at once, and with perfect efficacy, by not allowing any investigation. . . . If all criminals of every class had assembled and framed a system after their own wishes, is not this rule the very first which they would have established for their security? Innocence never takes advantage of it; innocence claims the right of speaking, as guilt invokes the privilege of silence.

Moreover, he pointed out, the rules applied by English courts do not in fact play fair, because the accused is not able to prevent his written words, or his conversations recounted by other witnesses, from being admitted as evidence:

> Thus, what the technical procedure rejects is his own evidence in the purest and most authentic form; what it admits is the same testimony, provided that it be indirect, that it has passed through channels which may have altered

it, and that it be reduced to the inferior and degraded state of hearsay.

His views have been endorsed by Salmond and Sir James Stephen, who wrote:

> I am convinced by much experience that questioning, or the power of giving evidence, is a positive assistance, and a highly important one, to innocent men, and I do not see why in the case of the guilty there need be any hardship about it.

Recently Sir John Foster, Q.C., M.P., told a Committee on the Preliminary Examination of Criminal Offences organized by *Justice:*

> An argument was put forward that it was bad luck on inexperienced offenders who often did not know their rights and gave themselves away, while the old lags, knowing they need not say anything, remained silent and secured acquittals. I would have thought that the bad luck was on the community that a sentimental sporting rule for which there was no justification should enable guilty men to escape.

He went on to claim that if the English rules had been applied at the Nürnberg Trial, not one of the defendants would have been convicted. Revocation of them, he argued, would make the English criminal trial 'less of a game or a contest and more of a serious inquiry as to the true nature of the crime and its real perpetrator'; it would even operate to the benefit of a defendant because 'if he has to go into the box the whole truth is more likely to emerge, which may throw light on some feature of the case and possibly lead to an acquittal or a diminution of the gravity of the offence (e.g. from capital murder to murder or manslaughter) or to the establishment of some mitigating factors'. This fuller picture would, at the least, give the

Judge the maximum material to help him to be able to award the most constructive sentence.

The abandonment of this rule would not be the innovation that its supporters assert. Already people are liable to be convicted if they refuse to disclose information concerning offences under the Official Secrets Acts, or even if they do not divulge who was driving their car at the time a road traffic offence was committed. If the principle is acceptable in these cases, it is strange that it is not thought 'sporting' in cases of armed robbery or murder. Dr Glanville Williams, who is a powerful advocate for the abandonment of the rule, believes it would not be necessary to have any penalty for refusal to answer; he would only require an accused person to listen to questions put to him by counsel for the prosecution. Some people believe that the defendant should also disclose in advance of his trial any alibi which he is going to claim (as he is obliged to in several U.S. States), in order that the police have a chance to investigate it and either to admit its validity or call evidence to disprove it.

If questioning was transferred to the public court in this way, it might be unnecessary to admit as evidence any statements whatever obtained by the police – which would thus remove from the arena a major source of dispute. Sir Patrick Hastings said that 'voluntary statements' are never voluntary, and should never be admitted in evidence. Most people are in a very frightened state at a police station. Even voluntary incriminating parts of statements have been known to be demonstrably wrong. Sympathy, anxiety, silence, exhaustion, bluff, cajolement, insinuation (and especially the alternation of these pressures) can, according to psychiatrists, eventually lead almost anybody to say what he thinks his listener wishes to hear. In India, following a period of disquiet about confessions, the British in 1872 introduced a new Evidence Act which has been retained since Independence. This permits the police to interrogate for purposes of investigation, but does not allow any resulting statement to be admitted in court. Instead, statements which will be admitted may be made at any time before a magistrate. Lord Shawcross, among others, has lately suggested the adoption of a similar practice here, but one eminent jurist with great experience of its working in India comments: 'There was always the suspicion that the confessing accused had been threatened or cajoled into making a confession, and tutored as to the answers he was to give when asked by the magistrate why he wishes to confess.' A policeman, who has lately returned from there, says succinctly that 'third degree used to go on while the magistrate was asked to wait'.

From this it is plain, not that the principle is necessarily wrong, but that the safeguards are not enough. 'The ideal,' Lord Devlin has stated, 'is an impartial investigator whose only duty is to bring the true facts to light.' Can we expect policemen, whom we require to be ardent in the pursuit of criminals, also to fulfil this role?

Provided safeguards are indisputable, there is no conflict between police efficiency and civil rights. The reverse is true – one of the civil liberties is freedom from violence and crime. Every civilized society must have powers to protect itself from destroyers. If properly exercised, these powers in themselves add to the maintenance of civilization and the true freedom of the individual. The police ought not to be handicapped in their efforts to prevent or detect crime while the criminal has every modern method at his disposal. There is a natural reluctance – especially a political one, which we shall meet again in the next chapter – to alter or increase the powers of the police. But their present situation is unsatisfactory on every count; it is anomalous and indefinite, as well as exposing them to damaging disputes. The police should not be in a position which causes them to complain about an increase in knowledge of the law. It is even worse – just as many people believe that in America the Fifth Amendment is responsible for condonation of third-degree methods – when the ineffectiveness of their legal powers compels the police themselves to ignore the law.

CHAPTER 4

National or Provincial?

Many people in this country are not aware that our police are still divided into 158 independent forces, each with a Police Authority (known as the Watch Committee in boroughs and cities, the Police Committee in counties) and each with its own C.I.D.

British suspicion of a national police force is an old one, recently reinforced by the experiences of Germany and Russia. Originally it found its roots in our xenophobia: early opponents continually muttered about Fouché, Naples, or Austria. 'Since we are so happy,' Cibber said in 1739, 'as not to have a certain power amongst us which in another country is called the police, let us rather bear this insult than buy its remedy at too dear a cost.' For a long time we refused to admit any word which meant 'police' into our English language. Even after we had adopted the French word the *British Magazine* in 1763 was writing: 'From an aversion to the French . . . and something under the name of police being already established in Scotland, English prejudice will not soon be reconciled to it.'

How valid is this feeling today? It is difficult to forget that Goering wrote in *Germany Reborn*:

> It seemed to me of the first importance to get the weapon of the police firmly into my own hands. Here it was that I made the first sweeping changes. Out of 32 police chiefs I

removed 22. Hundreds of inspectors and thousands of police sergeants followed in the course of the next month.

It was only because this had first been done that Hitler was able to use his gangs to establish a dictatorship as Dr Goodhart described. Similarly, when the communists seized power in Czechoslovakia in 1948, their first demand was for control of the police force. Yet, in fact, the Nazi Gestapo and *Schutzstaffeln*, the Tsarist Ochrana, the Soviet Cheka, Ogpu, and N.K.V.D., and the Fascist Ovra were all political and not civil police forces. Several Western European countries which are far from totalitarian possess national police forces, although most of them are of a somewhat smaller size than Britain. In the United States, the Federal Bureau of Investigation is virtually the only police force which is not tainted by politics. The Willink Commission in 1962 was unanimous in coming to the conclusion that the creation of a national police service would not be either 'constitutionally objectionable or politically dangerous'. They stated that the stigma of a 'police state' derives, not from a nationally organized police force, but from the totalitarian nature of a government which if it came to power 'would without doubt seize control of the police however they might be organized.' Dr Goodhart added: 'The danger in a democracy does not lie in a central police that is too strong, but in local police forces that are too weak.'

People who fear a national force here because of the risk of its political abuse overlook the fact that the government already has control of a quarter of the police, concentrated strategically in London. A government which wished to would be able to arrest the opposition's M.P.s by means of the Metropolitan Force. In addition, they would have under their control the main Special

Branch, which is the nearest equivalent we have in this country to a 'political police'.[1]

The real safeguard of a democracy is the accountability of its government to a freely elected Parliament. The new Police Bill shrunk from implementing the main recommendation of the Royal Commission, that the Home Secretary and the Secretary of State for Scotland should be made fully responsible in Parliament for their respective country's police. The result of the present situation was described by some witnesses to the Commission:

> The present fiction that, because he (The Home Secretary) does not control them (police forces), he should not be answerable for them seems to result in us having the worst of both worlds, in that control is in fact exercised by anonymous Home Office officials whose conduct cannot be examined or questioned.

The Home Office, for example, at present sends out over a hundred circulars annually to chief constables, which neither Parliament has any means of discussing nor local Councils any right to see. There is no subject of greater importance for Parliament to discuss than the police. The Ministers of Education and Health are answerable to M.P.s for matters in their fields, despite the autonomy of their departments locally; but the Home Secretary is not responsible for any police forces outside the Metropolitan area. The most he can do is to ask for a report, which leads to the anomaly that he can be effectively questioned about

[1] The plain-clothed man standing by Passport Control at London Airport, for example, is a Special Branch detective. His duty is 'to keep watch on any body of people, of whatever political complexion, whose activities seem likely sooner or later to result in open acts of sedition or disorder'. Since their formation in 1884 to deal with Fenians, they have successively watched Anarchists, Suffragettes, Germans, Indian Nationalists, the I.R.A., Fascists, and Communists.

a police matter which happens to take place for example in Dagenham, but not about one in Hornchurch, because that falls just the other side of the boundary of the Metropolitan Police Area.

When Mr Brooke declined the proposal of the Royal Commission that he should be fully answerable to Parliament for the police, he stated that he could not have the 'responsibility without the power'. He was unwilling to take the necessary power presumably because to do so was instinctively unacceptable politics to a Conservative cabinet. The root of the difficulty is how to reconcile Parliamentary ability to control the police with safeguards which would prevent any possible abuse from governmental direction. If this problem proves, as Mr Brooke apparently found, insoluble, the alternatives are to transfer either the responsibility or the direction of the police to a department which is separate from the central government.[1] One suggestion is to give the responsibility for the police to somebody from outside politics who is acceptable to all parties, such as an Ombudsman.

The present compromise solution is to diffuse the power between many different hands. The political justification for our fragmentary system of organization is that it provides a number of independent chief constables and police forces who can act as counterbalancing checks to the government's control of the Metropolitan force. If the police were reorganized in regional units, which most people think would also result in greater efficiency, the same safeguard would remain. But before examining the

[1] This is attractive on other grounds: the Home Secretary's job in any event has already become far too large for one man. When he has to consider whether to reprieve the murderer of a policeman, for example, his dual responsibilities for mercy and the police place him in an impossible conflict.

arguments for or against any form of unification, we must first see how true it is that, as one chief constable said, 'we are much more nationalized now than people think, only we don't call it that'.

The process of uniting the police in this country began very slowly, apart from Peel's foresight in making the Metropolitan Police area so large. A Select Committee, with Peel himself as chairman, had reported in 1822 that:

> it is difficult to reconcile an effective system of police with that perfect freedom of action and exemption from interference which are the great privileges and blessings of Society in this country, and Your Committee think that the forfeiture or curtailment of such advantages would be too great a sacrifice for improvements in police, or facilities in detection of crime, however desirable in themselves if abstractly considered.

Although another committee under Edwin Chadwick recommended the union of county police forces in 1839, they remained independent of central control. But in 1856 the Government was given powers to inspect them, in return for a financial grant of half the expenditure of each force. The number of Inspectors remained at three, and the annual inspections of some 200 forces were consequently cursory, up to 1945. But it was the other side of the bargain, the grant, which proved to be the Trojan horse, and it remains the greatest weapon of the Home Office today. As the cost of the police grew, the Home Secretary found that his power to withhold the government's contribution was pressure that no local authority could withstand. Grants have been withheld from Police Authorities on four occasions since 1945 (the last being in 1957): each time the desired result was soon obtained. The threat alone has generally proved sufficiently effective.

But the remedy (though not uncharacteristic of this country) is a blunt one. The cure is worse than the ailment: it could result in chaos for a district which is only incompetent, and if the local Authority refused to appoint any police force at all, there would be nothing the Home Secretary could do.

The next major advance was in 1919, when the Home Secretary acquired powers in the 'policeman's Magna Carta' to regulate pay, clothing, and conditions of service, although attempts to standardize criminal records were not made until just before the Second World War. The Home Office now also provides certain 'common services' for all forces, including, for example, nine regional forensic science laboratories, and the Police College at Bramshill. The Royal Commission urged that the policy and standards of recruitment, which are at present decided by each separate force, should also be centrally organized. In addition, many police would prefer that other facilities, such as detective training and driving schools, had a common standard by being provided centrally or regionally.

The pattern of the Home Secretary possessing in practice far more control than he is accustomed to acknowledge publicly is shown in the method of the appointment of chief constables. Technically, this is the prerogative of each Police Authority, but the Home Secretary must approve, and consequently can veto, every selection. One result has been that he is now able to impose a national policy that no chief constable shall be appointed who either comes from outside the police service, or who has spent a career in the force to which he has been appointed chief constable.

The new Police Bill has left the local Police Authorities with very few powers, other than financial control over the number of men and the equipment for their local force. Some boroughs are proud of the economy with which they run their police. The budgets certainly vary considerably: Sunderland, for example, spent £26 per 1,000 population in 1962–3 on police transport, compared with Pembrokeshire's £167 or Southend's £148. Borough forces are at an additional disadvantage compared with county ones, because Watch Committees' budgets, unlike those of county Police Committees, suffer further pruning at the hands of the borough Council's Finance Committee. In 1963, for instance, the chief constable of Stockport asked for 90 more men; the Watch Committee approved an increase of 47, but the Finance Committee allowed only 28. Councils at the present time are under strong pressure to pare down their rates generally. It is wrong that essential services, such as the police or education, should be in any way dependent on local wealth or politics. Rates may be a healthier form of taxation than the penalizing of earnings, but even though it is particularly appropriate to finance the police who protect property by means of them, there would be a clear gain from allocating the budget according to a national plan.

THE CASE FOR THE
PRESENT SYSTEM OF LOCAL FORCES

'Doubtless all arbitrary powers, well executed, are the most convenient, yet let it again be remembered that delays, and little inconveniences in the forms of justice, are the price that all free nations must pay for their liberty in more substantial matters.' Blackstone with these words was justifying complacency about our legal system, but they equally explain our instinctive aversion to a national police force. Democratic control, once it is lost, cannot be regained without a terrible struggle. Chinese people say, 'He who goes for a ride on a tiger can never get off'. But the present system of 158 separate police forces in this country continues because of enthusiasm for local control, as well as fear of central domination. At a time when administration seems to be increasingly impersonal, local police forces give people a chance of participation – and in a field where personal relationships are vital for the success of the police themselves. Any institution, like the jury, which enables people to feel that they are helping to govern as well as being governed should be welcomed. Not only are people able to gain civic experience on local Police Authorities, but to be self-policing is one of the eventual ideals of an open society.

If the case for the present system is accepted, as it was by the majority of the Royal Commission, there is equally an argument for extending it to the Metropolitan area, which is the only one in the country that does not have any democratic Police Authority. Hitherto this has been opposed on the grounds that its boundaries differ from those of the L.C.C., but in the future they will be virtually co-terminous with those of the new Greater London Council. Londoners at present have no say in the police rate in the Metropolitan area. This is the heaviest in the country, partly because Scotland Yard subsidizes other areas. If the Metropolitan Police were brought under either the G.L.C. or a special *ad hoc* Police Committee of the London Borough Councils, Scotland Yard's national services might be transferred to the Home Office. An additional reason for this change is that the present large Metropolitan bureaucracy suffers from having no liaison with the London public. Parliament cannot be said to exercise the democratic control over the Metropolitan force that a local Police Authority would: occasionally it finds time to discuss a complaint, but it is never able to consider questions of general policy. Some police officers think that the Metropolitan area is too large and unwieldy altogether.[1]

Sixty-four per cent of policemen interviewed were in favour of the present system of local forces, compared with 30 per cent who preferred a regional system and 6 per cent who wanted a national force. Chief constables, with very few exceptions, want to preserve local forces. One of them in the West Country said: 'It is an interesting trend today to push ultimate responsibility higher and higher. Having watched and participated in central and local government, I am certain that the individual gets a better crack of the whip at a local level, where a certain amount of flexibility can be used, than he will get from central government where all decisions are reached on rigid principles.' Although Dr Goodhart and Col. St Johnston argue that local associations will continue even if the police are re-organized on a regional basis, there remains in the minds of councillors a dread of larger bureaucratic control. (To other people it may seem little different from local bureaucratic control.) In the same way as neither the Home Secretary nor Parliament can dismiss a chief constable, equally they are unable to prevent one from acting in an improper way that falls short of illegality or inefficiency. There is no power to stop a chief constable from using objectionable methods or political discrimination – perhaps resulting from unconscious prejudices. Fortunately, however, examples of this type of complaint are extremely rare;

[1] It is interesting that the Metropolitan Commissioner is paid £7,000 a year, compared with £5,000 for his immediate superior, the Home Secretary.

and although local tyranny is no less obnoxious to those affected by it, it is unlikely to last so long as a national one – because in the last resort it is easier to correct. Since there cannot be too much protection, the ideal solution might be to have it at both local and Parliamentary level.

A separate criticism of the new Police Authorities established by the Police Bill is that many people feel it is quite wrong for magistrates, who must always appear impartial, to be members of them. Others criticize the weak control that is exercised by some Authorities: this may be the result of a general lack of informed public interest in the police and their problems. 'I think the present idea that we have local control of the police is a constitutional sham. All that can be said for the present system is that it is not centrally controlled. It is certainly not locally controlled,' T. L. Iremonger, M.P. has said. 'The Standing Joint Committees are able to exercise no democratic control because they meet so rarely,' declared one man who served on a County Council for twenty-five years. A Councillor who is also a M.P. added: 'Watch Committees do not even know what limited powers they have, and are afraid to exercise any. They never see the Inspector or his reports, and so don't get any adequate information.'

Local authorities, on the other hand, oppose any move towards unification because of fear that it would result in less good police service in their district. They argue that competition between chief constables has a healthy effect. (It is also true that one recent case of corruption in a police force only came to light because the railway police, who were making their own independent inquiries, became suspicious when they failed to receive any co-operation.) To set against the undeniable economies in overheads and equipment which amalgamations would produce, the Association of Municipal Corporations have produced figures which show that, in the years 1959–61, smaller urban forces had the most successful record of detection:

Number of men in city and borough forces (England and Wales)	Average percentage of detection of crime known
under 200	60%
200–349	56%
350–499	51%
500–1000	48%
over 1000	38%

These figures, however, may well prove nothing more than the fact that policing grows harder as the size of an urban area increases.

As in many other matters concerning the police, so little research has been done that it is common to find the same arguments being used by both sides. The supporters of small forces claim that the fact that their chief constable is able to know personally all the men under his command benefits morale and promotion; their opponents claim it has just the opposite effect. Many of the more ambitious policemen would welcome a unified force because of its increased opportunities for promotion: 'Those who want to stay local, can,' one constable said, 'while the others are able to get on.'

There is similar dispute about the effect on recruiting. One side argues that loyalty to the local force stimulates recruiting, and that a man from Anglesey, for instance, would hesitate before joining the Gwynedd force because of uncertainty where he might be posted. The other side say that national recruiting would be better than the present position, where, they claim, good recruits are being lost who are unsuccessful in joining their local force, yet still may be better than those who are being accepted elsewhere. (The present system of separate recruitment has resulted in some cases of a police constable who has been discharged by one force being taken on by another.) Forces in the north-east of England at the moment have their full establishment and to spare, whilst many of those in the south-east have long lists of vacancies.

THE CASE FOR UNIFICATION

Those who want a unified force deny that it would mean that any police officer would be transferred across the country unless he wished. They argue that a different chain of command need not affect local traditions: in Durham and Lancashire, for example, the divisional superintendents have always been encouraged to work as closely as possible with their own neighbourhoods. The gain in operational efficiency, the reformers claim, would be enormous. Not only would it cure the problem of the inadequate capital and specialist facilities of fragmented forces, but it would also obviate the difficulties and friction caused by their boundaries. They argue that the modern development of criminal organization and transport has now made further police reform necessary, in the same way as the Industrial Revolution eclipsed the parish constable system. This view repeats once more the words of the earlier reform, contained in the preamble to the 1829 Metropolitan Police Act:

> The local establishments of nightly watch and nightly police have been found inadequate to the prevention and detection of crime, by reason of the frequent unfitness of the individuals employed, the insufficiency of their number, the

limited sphere of their authority, and their want of connexion and co-operation with each other.

Liaison between separate forces can never, one chief constable argues, be as effective as command. Another one, who would like to see a unified force introduced immediately and not gradually built up, says that most forces do co-operate but that a few cases of personal friction can destroy the whole system. Detective officers in some forces are reluctant to share criminal information which they may depend on for their promotion. (Others have been known to deposit drunks over the boundary of the neighbouring force, in the same way as the old parish constable used to drive vagabonds into the next parish.)

The Secretary of the Scottish Police Federation, who in 1963 said that he would like one unified force for the whole of Scotland in place of the present 33, pointed out that its size would be roughly the same as the national Danish or Irish forces, and still less than half the Metropolitan establishment.

Fragmentation in England is seen at its worst in Lancashire, which has seventeen separate forces, fourteen of which are smaller than the Royal Commission's minimum size: some parts of the territory where the County Force operate are entirely cut off from the rest of their territory. At Stockport, Birmingham, and Hove one side of certain streets are in one police area and the other in another. In other parts of England, firms who wish to transport a valuable consignment have to notify over a dozen different police headquarters. Increasingly, criminals appear to be taking advantage of police boundaries in order to delay pursuit: detectives say that any of those who live in the London area only operate outside, and vice versa. When there was a robbery recently on a train between London and Brighton, it had to be investigated by four separate police forces – and it is still unsolved.[1]

Many policemen talk of a national force as being inevitable one day. Two chief constables said they thought that the next Royal Commission would recommend it. When a leader-writer in *The Times* recently wrote that 'whatever Dr Goodhart may recommend, the country is not likely to have a national police force within the foreseeable future', Dr Goodhart tartly replied, 'What is the "foreseeable future" depends, of course, upon one's capacity for foresight.'

Several members of the Willink Commission seem to have been attracted by the arguments in favour of a national force (two or three might have signed Dr Goodhart's minority Report if it had been written earlier). The Report of the majority was not strictly accurate when it said that they had received no evidence that the present system of local forces was a handicap to the police in dealing with crime: the Chief Constable of Lancashire, the Police Federation, the Magistrates' Association, and the Law Society amongst other witnesses urged reorganization. The *non sequiturs* in the majority's arguments were fully exposed by Dr Goodhart; but what they obviously felt was that a national force is at the moment politically impossible. The Association of Municipal Corporations has very strong influence inside Parliament: it would be as much as some borough M.P.s' seats are worth for them to support Dr Goodhart. A referendum alone could show whether the ordinary population (who may prefer effi-

---

[1] This country is, however, fortunate compared with the United States, where the fission of forces reaches its ultimate absurdity. In that country, 40,000 separate police administrations, with an average strength of only five men each, overlap each other at six levels.

ciency) are as opposed to a national force as the councillors.

It is a debatable point whether it is the duty of a Royal Commission to advocate only what is politically possible, or whether it should advance an ideal solution even though it believes it is unattainable. Dr Goodhart obviously subscribes to the latter view. Perhaps he was conscious of the development of organized crime in his home country of America; perhaps he was less blinkered by tradition, and was aware that in recent reorganization of the armed forces regiments and even the three services are being unified to meet modern conditions. But the other members of the Willink Commission who signed the majority Report, in deciding to work from the old rather than to build a new system, were not just being British or pre-occupied by history. They may have been canny enough to realize that if they compromised some very necessary reforms would make their way into a Police Bill, whereas if they created a new Jerusalem it would be likely to remain for ever in a pigeon-hole.

There are three future directions for reorganization, short of establishing a national force. First, by the unification of the C.I.D.) and also perhaps of the traffic police); second, by complete regroupment on a regional basis; or third, by amalgamation among the existing forces.

A NATIONAL C.I.D.

The first plan would form one separate national detective force (similar to the F.B.I., all of whose men are graduates (to wage war on crime, while uniformed forces remained locally organized. In this way, it is argued, the police could combine the advantages of both worlds: more efficient and specialized organization where it is most needed, while retaining the local tradition and contacts of the men on the beat. A nucleus for this force already exists in the Flying Squad at Scotland Yard. In 1962 the Yard co-operated with other forces in over 1,700 cases – an increase of nearly 500 on the record figure of the previous year. Reformers would like any big crime to be investigated automatically by national detectives: sometimes when, as at present, they have to wait to be called in until the local force has failed, the trail is three days cold. In France, besides a *brigade mobile* flying squad who can go anywhere, there are agents in every provincial centre under the control of the Sûreté Nationale. Sir Ronald Howe suggests that a national C.I.D. here with their headquarters perhaps at Birmingham could have had 500 detectives searching for a hide-out within three hours of the big mail train robbery. Their operations, like those of the F.B.I., might be restricted to the more serious crimes that are organized across the boundaries of police districts, and which are increasing in number and seriousness. Numerically, 80 per cent of the total number of crimes are estimated still to be 'local' ones. It would therefore be necessary also to have local detectives – ground-roots play an essential part in detection: basically, a good detective officer is very often a man who succeeds in collecting information, which in turn depends on local knowledge and contacts. Detectives will always need to rely on the rest of the police to act as their eyes and ears. Critics of a national C.I.D. say that a hybrid system would inevitably cause more friction than there is sometimes at present between the C.I.D. and the uniformed branch. Only 8 per cent of policemen who were questioned said that they wanted a national C.I.D., although another 24 per cent would like regional C.I.D.s.

There is a separate case for recruiting for the detective

branch to be distinct from that for other policemen. Criminals, who need no physical specifications, are often able to recognize our detectives by their height.[1] Professional opinion is divided on this subject. Some forces say that it is useful to be able to return unsuccessful detectives to the uniformed branch; their opponents reply that this is too much the civil-service or trades-union attitude, and that they should be dismissed. According to them, a detective needs specialized qualities because he is working against the minds of criminals, whereas the uniformed man works among the law-abiding public. One chief constable, an exceptional and humane man, argued that here lay just the danger. He said that detective officers who shared a criminal culture for too long can become too 'C.I.D.-minded'.[2] He emphasized that it is more important for them to be better human beings than to be better detectives: he has a policy of automatically returning C.I.D. officers, when they are promoted, back to work in the uniformed branch for two or three years.

A NATIONAL TRAFFIC FORCE

One problem which is certain to increase in the future is the number of traffic offenders. In 1962 nearly a million

[1] Some of the most brilliant French dectives, who are selected for their ability separately from the police, are not only tiny but also have glasses and flat feet, and would stand no chance before a selection board in this country.

[2] The 1929 Royal Commission said some similar words: 'Some of the C.I.D. (Scotland Yard) evidence which we have heard leaves a somewhat disquieting impression upon our minds. There is, we fear, a tendency among this branch of the service to regard itself as a thing above and apart, to which the restraints and limitations placed upon the ordinary police do not, or should not, apply. This error, if not checked, is bound to lead to abuses which may grow until they bring discredit upon the whole police force.'

motorists were prosecuted in this country, and the number
of vehicles is officially expected to double in the next
decade and treble by the decade following. The harm they
cause is even greater than that due to criminals: every
second of the day, careless motorists are estimated to be
doing £430 of damage. A person is injured on the roads
every 94 seconds, and another is killed every 78 minutes –
over forty times the number of people who are murdered.
74,000 uninsured motorists came to light in 1962 only
because they were involved in accidents. American studies
suggest that 19 out of 20 traffic offences at present escape
detection.[1]

New Zealand has recently formed a separate force of
300 traffic policemen. Dr Goodhart argues that it would
be easy to recruit drivers for a similar body here. Other
people support the idea on the grounds that it would hive
off a great deal of public resentment from the rest of the
police.

The idea of special motor-patrols by the police, whose
object was to give advice rather than to prosecute, was
tried out by the Home Office in 1938. In the districts
where they were used, they resulted in a decrease of 6·7
per cent in fatalities during the trial period, compared
with an increase of 3·4 per cent in the districts not
operating the scheme; during the same period they prosecuted 12 per cent fewer people, compared with the other
areas where prosecutions increased by 5 per cent. But
police officers say that it would be a wasteful duplication
of manpower to have a completely segregated traffic

[1] Despite these figures, radar speed checks are still looked upon as
'unsporting': this seems a relic of the attitude which caused the motoring organizations to be founded partly so that they could give warning
of police patrols.

police force looking for only one type of offender. The man on traffic patrol deals with crime as much as with traffic: not only are 70,000 cars stolen every year, but vehicles are estimated to be employed in between 25 per cent and 50 per cent of serious crimes. Moreover, a recent study by Terence Willett showed that the anti-social motorist and the criminal overlap to a surprising degree. 23 per cent of the people convicted of serious driving offences in one area also had a record of having committed other crimes, and a further 9 per cent were 'known to the police'. Four out of five of those charged with causing death by dangerous driving, and 78 per cent of those caught driving while disqualified, had criminal records.

Although there is a clear case for more police patrol cars on the roads, their segregation into an entirely separate force is not desirable. A lifetime spent only in this unpopular work would have a doubtful effect on a man's morale, and there is also a danger that the force might develop into a 'sub-police' which possessed inferior authority and respect.

REGIONAL FORCES

As an alternative to these specialized departments being co-ordinated vertically, the existing police forces could regroup themselves regionally. There are many signs that the pressure towards unification is having results in this direction. Experiments have been made in combined units to patrol motorways, and crime squads on the pattern of the London Flying Squad have been started in Newcastle, Manchester, Liverpool, Bristol, Nottingham, and Birmingham. In addition, occasional *ad hoc* crime units are formed to deal, for example, with a particular gang which operates in three counties. It is likely that regional crime units (the word 'Squads' has perhaps unhappy effects) will gradually be established all over the country by forces who are anxious to demonstrate that they can liaise, as the price for retaining their independence.

During the Second World War the emergency conditions showed how creaky the local system was and brought about a form of regional organization. 21 amalgamations took place, and the remaining police forces were fitted into eleven Civil Defence regions. Today, a greater degree of co-ordination would in particular be welcomed by those who are the victims of 'commercial crime': security officers of companies wish that movements of valuable consignments could be planned at regional levels. One firm, which has had £1 million's worth of its goods hi-jacked over the past five years, said that co-operation between some police forces is nominal and that only lip-service is as yet paid to regional crime units. Part of the trouble is that the knowledge that the police possess is often so fragmented that it loses its value. One ex-inspector said, 'The average copper is most reluctant to give away to his superiors and lazy comrades what he had, by years of practice studded with complaints to answer, learned the hard way for himself.' This applies even more between different forces, who are each striving to improve their clear-up rate in relation to those of their neighbours.

Local government and planning in Britain is increasingly moving in a regional direction. We seem to be developing a three-tier form of government; the police might perhaps best be organized in the middle (regional) tier. In this way it would be possible to retain in the reorganization the benefits of local liaison committees, though members could not be expected to travel long distances to regional meetings without payment. England and Wales are already divided into nine Police Districts, and there are regional forensic laboratories in London, Birmingham, Bristol, Cardiff, Harrogate, Nottingham, Preston, and Newcastle. There may be far-reaching effects from the recent appointment of an Inspector of Constabulary to each Police District (other than London), and the building of a permanent office for him in his territory.

AMALGAMATIONS

As a stage towards regional union, the police are likely to see an increasing number of forces amalgamated in the next few years. This has been pressed as a matter of growing urgency by many committees during the last fifty years. In 1860 there were 226 separate forces in England and Wales; in 1939 there were 183; by 1949 this was reduced to 129. Today there are 125, with another 33 in Scotland. The size of their establishments ranges from 18 men in the Shetland Islands to the Metropolitan's 20,166. Only some 44 forces are above the strength of 500 men which the Royal Commission said was the 'optimum' size. (Sir Henry Willink has since stated that he personally regards a force of 1,000 as the figure to be aimed at.) 68 forces – almost half – are smaller than the strength of 350 which the Commission found to be 'justifiable only in special circumstances'. Notwithstanding the evidence, new County Boroughs are as anxious to have their own police forces as independent nations are to possess their own airlines. Since the last war Bournemouth has added a new force of its own, and in April 1964 Luton started yet another separate one which will halve the Bedfordshire force of 600, against the advice of both the Police Federation and the Home Secretary.

For many years people have been urging that it is archaic for the City of London to have its own force, and that it should be merged with the rest of London.[1] The present force, which is entirely surrounded by the Metropolitan area, owes its origin to the historical accident of Peel having to concede it to the City caucus in order to save his projected New Police from an early Parliamentary death. The usual excuse for preserving the separate force is that the City population floods in during the day and out again at night, so that the position there is the opposite of the rest of London. But surely this tidal flow would equally help a combined police force? The extra officers who are necessary for traffic control during the day could economically be used at other times wherever they were most needed.

It is unfortunate that the Police Bill did not include the Royal Commission's recommendation to set up an amalgamating commission 'as a matter of urgency'. Instead the Government stated that they prefer to await the local government area review which is slowly examining the whole country (though hope of decisive action from this quarter was not encouraged by Sir Keith Joseph's capitulation to Rutland). The re-drawing of the boundaries of police areas, when it does come, should be based on local conditions and conurbations, rather than on any rigid formula of size. In many ways it is disastrous for boroughs to be separated from their county hinterlands: hearts should be returned to their bodies.

Amalgamation eventually is likely to result in the 125 forces in England and Wales being pared down to 100, or

[1] In the same way that the Court of Common Council should be merged, not with a rich area like Westminster, but perhaps with Stepney.

more radically to 50 (based on counties) – perhaps ending as a logical conclusion in nine regions.

It is difficult to assess the relative merits of the alternative methods of reorganizing the police in the present absence of research, but an eventual regional structure seems the most likely direction of development. This would satisfy those people who feel that England's population is too large and diverse for one national force, and yet that county and borough forces are too fragmentary. Some boundary problems, it is true, would remain; but regions would probably be acceptable to those people who have a lingering political fear of one national force. It is not certain that they would necessarily be a halfway stage towards a national force: central control, in some ways, is easier to exercise over weak local forces than stronger regional ones.

CHAPTER 5

Manpower: Recruiting, Training and Career

When the Royal Commission on the Police recommended in their Interim Report on Pay in November 1960 a very substantial increase, it was widely assumed that the manpower problems of the force were very largely over, especially since the recommendation was implemented the following month. Unfortunately, three years later, at the end of October 1963, the force was still 7·2 per cent or 5,988 men under strength in England and Wales. In London the deficiency was 12·6 per cent, about half the national shortage, on an establishment which itself is a considerable underestimate of the needs of the Metropolis.

The authorized establishment in London has risen proportionately far more slowly than have those of the provincial forces. Home Office policy has been not to grant an increase in establishment to a force unless it has already almost reached its existing maximum. This has meant that in some areas, particularly in large conurbations where in absolute terms the shortage has been much greater, the establishment figure has become meaningless as an index of actual needs. Migration, both internal and from abroad, has also caused a disproportionate increase in the size of these large towns, and in many cases brought additional problems to their already overburdened police forces. Although actual strength throughout the country has increased by 7,000 in the last two and a half years, the Home Secretary has estimated that at least a further 10,000 men are needed, especially in cities.

Establishment figures are misleading, too, because by their very nature they can never be attained: since they cannot be exceeded, there will always be a slight deficiency owing to the time-lag between a man's leaving the force and his replacement. Similarly, neither establishment figures nor those of actual strength have taken into account the loss of manpower due to shorter hours, additional leave, and so on, which has accumulated over the years.

Figures of actual strength are little more meaningful. There is again the gap between 'men on paper' and men in fact. One harassed inspector in charge of a 10 p.m. to 6 a.m. shift commented, 'I've got an area here the size of a town like, say, Wolverhampton, and a lot of valuable property in it, and I've only got one man out. What am I supposed to do if anything happens and he gets tied up here with a prisoner or something? It's getting to the stage now when inspectors and sergeants are the only men out.' Such situations were by no means unusual in this force.

Essential, the problem is one of deployment of manpower as well as of an overall shortage. 'Men on paper' on such a typical occasion might number about six; but one would be away on a special duty in some other part of the city; one would have had to go off duty at 2 a.m. in order to be at court by 9.45 a.m. next morning (eight hours between shifts is a statutory requirement for the police); another would be an observer or driver on a night patrol car, or perhaps waiting in the station to drive the superintendent's car in case of emergency; and at least one further man would be having 'time off' for a sporting or social fixture connected with the force on the day following. It is not altogether unusual for a man to take part in three or four of these activities, which means that he is rarely available for a normal eight-hour tour of duty. Far from being good for morale, as is often claimed, this situation can have a very depressing effect on the men remaining, who know before they set foot outside the station that their task of protecting life and property single-handed in so vast an area is impossible.

Further aspects of the deployment of manpower concern policy at a more basic level. In Chapter 2 an example was quoted of a force which had greatly increased in size, but where the whole of this increase had been swallowed up in departments concerned with more specialized aspects of police work than beat patrol. This again affects morale, which is as important to efficient policing as actual numbers. With justification beat officers complain that though frequent lip-service is paid to their primary role as preventers of crime and liaison officers with the public, whenever a man is needed for some other task someone is taken off the beat to perform it.

In a rural area this problem takes a different form. Whereas men can be whittled away one at a time from a shift of several men in a city, a single man would be missed immediately from a residential beat station: a country beat officer cannot be transferred to another department if his beat would thereby be left vacant. The unpopular practice has therefore been adopted in some forces of posting men from country beat stations to work part-time in their divisional or sub-divisional headquarters. The men's claim that neither function can be properly performed in these circumstances is only partly justified. Much of the dissatisfaction arises from the autocratic manner in which such decisions are made; and much of it could be eliminated by a discussion between the men involved and their senior officers, so that each could appreciate more fully the problems of the other.

In one force where this occurred the main complaint of the men focused on the waste involved in travelling several miles to the divisional headquarters, for which no expenses were paid. Police time was allowed for cycling – in some cases as much as six miles each way – but no thought was given to the discomfort involved in this, the consequent loss of incentive to work on arrival, or the latent waste of paying highly trained men for time spent cycling to a given point (as distinct from conducting a cycle patrol). Thus, in this area in a period of three months, 37 per cent of the hours worked had been in the sub-divisional head-quarters. Since complete shifts were rarely worked in this way, they involved well over half the working days, when the constable considered that he should have been attending to the needs of his own 'patch'. Apart from the loss of man-hours on the beat, there is again the additional factor of slowly ebbing morale. These men were always faced with the temptation to throw in their hands on their own beats and do only what was essential – a normal reaction when one is faced with a task which cannot adequately be carried out in the time allotted. In addition they were made to feel by such requirements that their own beats were of little importance to their superiors, 'so why should I care?' It cannot be emphasized too often that hidden wastage of this kind is as disastrous for the police force as a whole as the more obvious deficiency in numbers.

RECRUITING

The Police Federation, chief constables, and others have repeatedly said that the lack of police manpower is not solely a result of low recruitment. In its Interim Report the Royal Commission stated: 'all the evidence indicates that the problem of manning the police is less a problem of recruitment than of unnecessary wastage'. This argument becomes clearer when one considers that in the year ending October 1963 the police recruited 5·9 per cent of their total strength establishment, more than sufficient men to replace the 'normal' wastage due to retirement on pension, death, or dismissal in the same year. Some 'abnormal' wastage for such reasons is unavoidable. The recruitment figures must, therefore, be high enough to compensate for this even when the present target of a new establishment figure has been achieved.

Since the announcement of the first police pay rise in 1960 recruiting has undoubtedly improved slightly, as the graph opposite shows. The monthly fluctuations remain, with a peak intake in the spring due to police recruitment policy and the ending of the financial year. The additional pay increase granted in September 1962 did not produce such a marked improvement, although the upward trend continued.

But the crucial questions are: who are these new recruits, and why do they join? More important than the problem of numbers, perhaps, is the quality of the intake. Viewed from this angle the picture is less encouraging. Since there is room in the force for men with a wide range of capabilities, the standards set for entry are necessarily minimal. Contrary to popular belief, a minor conviction does not necessarily disqualify a candidate, provided it is disclosed frankly. Height standards, as is well known, range from 6 ft to 5 ft 8 in., and there are similar variations in the requirements for chest measurement. But it is becoming increasingly realized that physical standards, other than

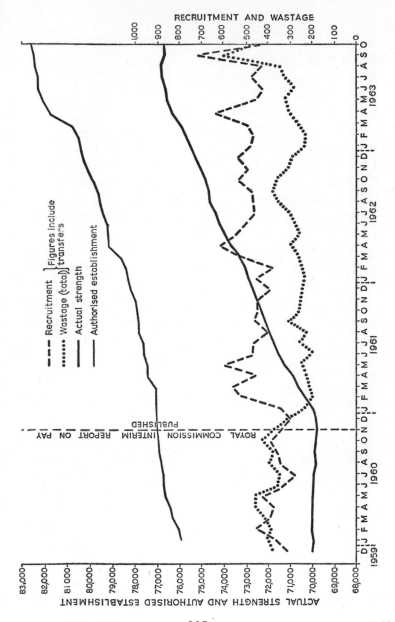

RECRUITMENT AND WASTAGE

ACTUAL STRENGTH AND AUTHORISED ESTABLISHMENT

- - - Recruitment ⎫ Figures include
········ Wastage (total) ⎬ transfers
——— Actual strength
——— Authorised establishment

ROYAL COMMISSION INTERIM REPORT ON PAY PUBLISHED

medical fitness, are of little relevance in much of modern police work. In fact, they are quite frequently waived in favour of a good candidate. Those who claim that the repeated lowering of the height standard is a major factor in the loss of public respect are harking after a vanished role. Such an attitude is not unusual. Throughout the service and in all ranks there can still be found many, perhaps a majority, with a basic suspicion of the 'book man'. Education is regarded as the antithesis of practicality and a mythical 'common sense'. 'He'd be no good in a scrap, what you want is someone who can get on with the job', is all too frequent a comment, and the suspect 'intelligentsia' of the force are required to prove their prowess before legitimate authority, as distinct from merely the power of rank, is attributed to them.

This attitude among the members of the police force themselves hinders the development of that favourable 'public image' which more insightful senior officers and the Federation realize is a pre-requisite for attracting sufficient recruits of the right type. Even today only 1 in 30 of the applicants to the Metropolitan Police is considered suitable.

In their own recruiting campaigns the police do little to aid the situation. Often their contact with schools, at careers conventions and similar occasions, is amateurish: there is little awareness of what is most likely to appeal to the high-minded sixth-formers whom the police themselves claim they want to attract. More than one case has been known where the adverse reactions of form-mates have prevented a bright child from following up his rashly announced intention of joining the police. This reaction is based, in an intelligent sixth form, on the notion that the choice is a shocking waste of brainpower. The weakness of the public image is obvious.

Nor do the recruiting advertisements and booklet help. These appear to be designed to appeal, above all, to the immature. Emphasis is on 'the spirit of adventure' rather than the 'spirit of service'. The poorly designed advertisement for a career in the Metropolitan Police which appears in the national newspapers claims that the police are 'right in the centre of things' and speaks more of the glamorous specialist departments than of the valuable services which can be performed in the course of twenty-five or thirty years' shift work on the beat. A considerable part of the wastage during the probationary period may result from recruits joining with this primary misconception about the nature of the work.

The booklet gives a similarly false picture. Again the emphasis is on the more spectacular aspects of police work. One caption reads: 'The police are turning out super-drivers to beat the car bandits'. More misleading, except to the very discerning, is the vague statement that 'a week-end off usually comes along periodically'. In fact, in those forces working a three-shift system where the additional four hours a week off duty has not yet become a reality, only one weekend in seven is free.

For women the advertising is somewhat better, and the social service aspect of the work is more emphasized. This, together with the quality of the serving police-women, must account for the rapid fading of the old stereotype of the masculine, muscular, harsh-voiced policewoman (who probably never existed).

Why, then, do young men join the police force? Without concrete evidence of differences between them and the rest of the population it is dangerous to speculate on possible psychological motives. Even if we knew of such differences, it would be unwise to assume that they were the cause rather than the effect of joining the police. Nowadays there is a newly developed tendency to empha- size the 'worthwhile job' aspect in the choice of a career – a concession to more general 'other-directedness'. In the pre-war years security and the relatively high pay were undoubtedly major reasons for joining. The climate of opinion was such that it was a fairly obvious choice for a man of the necessary physique. Then, as now, the social background of recruits was mainly social class III in the Registrar General's classification (i.e. skilled manual and low-grade non-manual workers). In a sample of policemen interviewed in the course of a survey carried out during 1962 and the early months of 1963, 60·1 per cent of the men fell into this category on the basis of parental occu- pation. The social class background of the city policemen interviewed was significantly higher than that of the man from a county force. 31·6 per cent of city men gave a parental occupation of social class II, compared with only 15·8 per cent of county men. For social class III the figures were 55·8 per cent and 71·9 per cent respectively. Few men in either force said that their origins were semi-skilled or unskilled working-class. The social background of the city wives was similar to that of their husbands, but in the county twice as many wives as men came from social classes IV or V, and only 48 per cent came from social class III.

One main source of recruitment which has now dried up was men leaving the army. At one time 50 per cent of the intake were men who had just completed their National Service. This is one reason why men at present serving in the police complain about the immaturity of the recruits: they forget that, apart from anything else, they tend to be a year or two years younger than their post-

National Service counterparts (the minimum age for joining is 19), and that in the course of this time they will 'grow up' anyway. There is also a widespread tendency among policemen to eulogize the armed services as a training ground for 'life', mainly perhaps because this forms part of their own experience in about 80 per cent of cases.

In the immediate post-war years the general housing shortage may have provided an incentive to join the police force, where nominally at least a house is guaranteed with the job. But it is doubtful if such a reason would be sufficient for a man who had no predisposition to join.

Today the security attraction is somewhat of a myth. Not only are the relative advantages as regards pension less great, but few of the men are able to face realistically at the outset of their serivce the problems involved in starting work in a new field at a minimum age of 44, and a maximum (for a constable) of 55. A Police Federation official commented, 'They think that when they leave this job the world will be waiting for them with open arms, and then they're disillusioned. They can never understand why people take up security jobs and the like, and then when they come to leave they find themselves forced to do the same thing.'

So far from being a secure job, for the county man police work has the built-in insecurity that he is faced at the end of his service with nowhere to live. Since a man may be required to move anywhere in the county during the course of his service, it is only in rare cases that the chief constable will give him permission to settle and buy a house. This largely accounts for the higher proportion of county men (54·6 per cent as against 32·6 per cent) who say that they intend to complete thirty years' service before retiring. Commutation of pension is not possible for those who retire after only twenty-five years, and for the county man this is essential to provide him, at the age of fifty or thereabouts, with the initial payment on a house.

Thus as the economic reasons for joining have increasingly little weight, there is a strong possibility that a more uniform type of personality will be recruited – men attracted solely by the appeal of the work itself. Just what this type will be it is for the police service to decide. At the moment there are dangers. As the Royal Commission pointed out, the police service offers more immediate, tangible power than the lower echelons of any other occupation. Coupled with this fact is the advertising campaign's emphasis on the *importance* of the position, rather than the work. The reader can decide for himself what type of young man is likely to respond to such appeals; whether he is more likely to be a dedicated public servant or an insecure young man seeking status through his uniform and, more dangerously, the exercise of a potentially autocratic power.

The Royal Commission also stated that the three essential requirements for a recruit are integrity, mental and physical fitness, and an adequate education. It is necessary to provide '(a) an adequate number of efficient policemen, and (b) sufficient young men of such ability and educational attainments as would fit them to occupy in due course the highest posts in the service'.

Integrity is a quality which cannot be assessed objectively in a recruit; physical standards have already been dealt with; there remain the educational requirements, which hitherto have varied widely from force to force, and in many cases have involved little more than the ability to pass a simple examination in the 'three R's' and an elementary general knowledge paper. All parties concerned are now agreed that the force would benefit from a national entrance examination, which would not only guarantee standards but serve further to improve the public's conception of the police service as a profession. Evidence to the Royal Commission was conflicting as to whether educational standards had been lowered to meet the need for manpower. Both the Home Office and the chief constable said they had not, but pointed out that this general standard did not constitute the crux of the problem. The real danger for the future of the force lay in the fact that so few of the entrants were potentially able to fill the need for future leaders. True, two fifths of the normal entry and half of the cadets have a grammar school education, whereas the national average is roughly one in three. But no more than 32 per cent of the normal entry had one or more passes at O-level. For the cadet entrants, 62 per cent of the men joining the Metropolitan Police were in this category, and 40 per cent of those joining provincial forces. But even a pass at O-level does not betoken a man of sufficient quality to become a leader in his profession. At the time the Commission sat, only 1 per cent of the normal intake in the provinces had two or more A-level passes, and 0 per cent of the cadets; equivalent figures for the Metropolitan Police were 2 per cent and 2·5 per cent. This suggests that the better promotion chances offered in the Metropolis, which will be considered later, attract men of higher calibre. It is considered, with reason, that part of the difficulty in attracting highly qualified recruits is the necessity of serving four years on the beat before the promotion examination can be taken; this entails a wait of at least five years before the promotion becomes effective. For an ambitious youngster joining at 19 this may be irksome, if reasonable. But such a structure is unlikely to attract the graduate entrants that the police claim they need. After three years living on a scholarship, and with the chance of a much higher immediate salary elsewhere in more congenial working conditions, together with long-term prospects which are at least as good, only a few graduates will opt for the police force; and not necessarily those who will make the best policemen.

A better alternative would be for the police force to arrange for a number of its most promising men to have leave of absence for three years to attend a university, on condition that they returned to serve an agreed minimum period with the force. If pay were continued at the normal rate during this time it would enable men with families, who might otherwise have slipped through the educational net, to take advantage of the scheme, and the period of absence would, of course, be counted as part of the men's service for pension purposes. This would give them an education both broader and deeper than any purely professional college could be expected to do. At the same time, the taint of 'officer caste' which rendered Hendon[1] so unpopular could be avoided.

One recent attempt to attract more suitable candidates to the force has been the introduction and rapid extension of the cadet scheme. Under this a youth may join the service at 16, on leaving school, and become a junior cadet, later becoming a senior cadet before joining the

[1] Hendon Police College was founded in 1933 by Lord Trenchard, then Commissioner of the Metropolitan Police. The aim was to create a special officer cadre for the service. The course was open to direct entrants, who numbered about one third of the students. Following intense opposition from the rest of the service it was disbanded on the outbreak of war in 1939. Twenty-six of the chief constables serving today passed through the Hendon College.

police force proper at the age of 19. Police cadets have now achieved full status, under the terms of the new Police Bill. They are a recognized part of the service and the responsibility of the chief constables and the Police Federation, rather than the local authority as hitherto. (This anomalous position had arisen because the cadet scheme developed from the practice of employing 'boy clerks', who were ultimately destined to become police officers, to work in station offices.) The aim of the scheme is to offer good career prospects to school-leavers before those who may be attracted to the police service have a chance to find a niche in industry. In most cases some attempt is made to give the cadet a certain amount of insight into normal civilian life. Periods of three months or so working in factories and at a variety of civilian tasks are therefore arranged. Doubtless now that the Federation is responsible for cadets plans for some standardization in training will be accelerated.

Although the fear that, as policemen, ex-cadets will have a less good rapport with the general public may to some extent be genuine, it does not wholly account for the intense opposition to cadets amongst serving policemen. Much of it is a rationalization: similar reasons are put forward for their opposition to the various schemes for quick promotion. Any policy change which seems to lay greater stress on 'book learning' as opposed to practical experience is seen as a threat, as implied denigration of the old 'hand down the collar and knock him off' skills. Increasingly those who practise them are being forced to realize that such skills are wholly inadequate, and understandably they resist this knowledge. Their myth of the old 'cuff on the ear' policeman has thus developed as a further bulwark against the encroachment of new insights in human relations and corresponding new methods of policing.

Official Federation policy is now that not more than one-third of the intake should be ex-cadets, in strong opposition to the policy of the Home Office, which considers an intake of 50 per cent from the cadets to be desirable, and the Metropolitan Commissioner who would prefer 66 per cent. As yet there is no need for fear in this respect. Only 24·71 per cent of recruits in the year ending October 1963 in England and Wales were ex-cadets.

One further aspect of recruitment remains to be considered. If recruitment is inadequate, why is it that there are no coloured regular recruits when the coloured community is now 1 per cent of the national population?[1] (There is at least one successful coloured prison officer.) The Federation says that it has no official policy on this matter. Others give as a reason either (a) that those coloured men who apply are below the normal standard for white recruits, or (b) that the general public are not yet ready to accept being policed by coloured men – never, be it noticed, is it mentioned that there would be internal difficulties, which is obviously the real case. If policemen comprise a typical cross section of the community, and are not in any way a selected group, one would expect to find among their numbers a considerable proportion who are prejudiced against coloured people, reflecting the present state of affairs in England. This is a fact which should not be hidden but faced squarely and a solution to it sought.

Despite the fact that there is already a coloured magistrate in England, the first of the above arguments is impossible to disprove, for no record is kept of unsuccessful

[1] There are two coloured *special* constables.

applicants for the various forces. One inspector did, however, put forward a reasonable case on similar grounds. His point was that the first coloured recruits would have to be very much above the normal standard, just as the early policemen had to be of outstanding calibre in order to counteract the prejudice of their day. As far as he knew, no such exceptional applicant had as yet presented himself.

The second argument has less validity. It is incumbent upon the police to lead in this respect, and not to follow public opinion. Coloured policemen would be no more generally unpopular today than were their white predecessors when they first went out into the streets of London in 1829; as in the earlier case, their task would be of undoubted difficulty, but not insurmountable. Some policemen use the subtle argument that coloured people are more popular through not having any police officers. One man said: 'We once had a Mohammedan, and we even have one or two Jews.' Others spoke candidly of their feeling on this matter, saying that it would lower the standing of their job; and one remarked, 'I wish people would stop all this hypocrisy about saying anyone can be a policeman. Of course there's a colour bar, but mainly I'd say because the general public won't stand for it.' He added, as a fervently expressed hope, 'It will probably come, but not in this generation.' In fact, the sooner it comes the sooner it will become accepted. Prejudice tends to grow by being pandered to. If the southern United States can accept coloured policemen, we can.

But this is not the place for an examination of the nature and bases of colour prejudice in this country. In any case, most of those who have advocated the use of coloured policemen have suggested that as a preliminary measure their work should be principally in coloured areas. This is not so much because 'white' people would resent them as because it is among coloured people that they can, for the moment, be of greatest value. Dr Michael Banton, of Edinburgh University, in an article in *The Police Chief* (an American magazine for police officers) has explained in some detail why this is so.[1] In brief, he states that a man's identification with his own community is much stronger, and that because of this identity a community confers only upon one of its own legitimate authority.

In their evidence to the Royal Commission the National Council for Civil Liberties recommended the immediate recruitment of a small number of coloured policemen. 'The matter has been discussed in responsible police circles, and we understand that there is a large minority view that recruitment should in fact start at once in the usual way.' They also recommend the use of coloured people in police stations on non-police tasks, but it seems doubtful whether this would overcome either internal or external prejudices. For both the public and the police the picture presented would be one of coloured people acting once again in a secondary and subordinate role. What might be a more useful idea would be to employ first a coloured woman police officer, who would thus have equal status with the 'white' officers, and be in a position to begin the uphill task of breaking the barriers of prejudice. She would have two advantages over a possible coloured male officer: in the first place prejudice is rooted largely in very irrational fears and sexual insecurity, so that there is in general less antagonism towards coloured women; secondly, those men who did

[1] *The Police Chief*, April 1963, pp. 8–20. (Official publication of the International Association of Chiefs of Police Inc.)

object to the employment of a coloured policewoman would be less likely to show their hostility overtly than in the case of a man – and since their work would be largely distinct, they would in any case have less opportunity for doing so. Coloured and white nurses manage to work amicably side by side in many of our hospitals, and we have no reason to suppose that policewomen are as a group any less tolerant.

PROMOTION

It has been suggested that two aspects of police structure are closely related to the type of recruit that is attracted to a police career. These are (a) promotion chances and (b) training, and they are, of course, connected. Before examining the system of promotion it is as well to remember the national picture of promotion opportunities. Eighty per cent of the total strength are constables, and a further 12 per cent are sergeants. Thus only 8 per cent of those recruited can reasonably expect to attain a senior rank. Yet it is in the recruiting of this 8 per cent that the greatest difficulty is experienced.

The promotion system is different in the Metropolitan Police from that in the rest of the country. In all forces a recruit must serve two years as a probationary constable after joining. The first promotion examination, that for a constable seeking promotion to sergeant, can be taken in both types of force after four years' service, that is at a minimum age of 23 years. A further examination is necessary before promotion to inspector is possible, and before sitting this the candidate must have been made a substantive sergeant. This means that actual promotion to inspector cannot, at a minimum, take place until after seven years' service. In effect, any graduate joining the force at 21 would have to wait until he were almost 30 before earning a salary in the range £1200–£1300, which he could achieve in a much shorter time in almost any other walk of life.

But, except in the Metropolitan Police, the length of service at which a man could qualify for promotion, and the length of service before he were actually 'made up', have in the past borne little relation to each other. The Metropolitan Police have for some years been operating their own system of promotion by examination, whereby a man can be promoted immediately on the basis of his results. Unlike the provincial forces, the Metropolitan Police conduct their own examinations. This speeds the process of promotion, and provides the more intelligent entrant with some guarantee that his claims or abilities will not be overlooked. For in provincial forces it has not only been the relative slowness of promotion which has deterred recruitment, but also the lack of certainty. Other factors than one's intellectual ability, which can neither be identified nor controlled, are suspected to influence selection for promotion.

To a large extent the degree of rationalization in the promotion system is a function of size, as one would expect. It is no accident that the largest force in the country was the first to develop a system of promotion by examination. At the other extreme, in the very small forces promotion still appears to be a very haphazard affair. In one force where 190 constables had served the minimum four years, 58·9 per cent of them were qualified for promotion to sergeant, and a total of 76·3 per cent of them had passed at least one paper. Of these same men, nine had been fully qualified before 1950, including three who qualified during the 1930s. The mean number of years which had elapsed since qualifying was 7·21, the range being from 0 to 29 years. It is understandable that in such circumstances there should be bitterness about promotion. The mean number of vacancies per annum from 1950 to 1959, before the Royal Commission Report could have any effect on retirement, was 3·5. Thus even if no further men were qualified in the meantime it would take 37·3 years for all these men to be promoted.

Apart from the recruiting problem which it is alleged such a situation can create, a far more insidiously dangerous effect is on the morale of the men involved. When there are too many good men for too few places, the selection for promotion must be based on estimate of some intangible merit. The men themselves refer cynically to this as the 'blue eyes and hair colour' basis of selection. Senior officers themselves will on occasion admit the personalized basis of the system. 'If I'm called out to a case', said one, 'and meet the beat man there and see he has done a good bit of work, then naturally I remember his name so when there's a vacancy for sergeant and everyone's saying what about so and so, I'll say "oh yes, I know him, he's a good bloke". Well, that's fair enough, isn't it?' Fair enough perhaps, but no one could deny that there are equally good men who never have the good fortune to attract attention in this way, and mistakes, of course, are similarly remembered. Almost every man can cite at least one such case of injustice which he has known, where a single error, borne in mind by a senior officer, has blocked promotion, at least until that senior officer retired.

Accusations of favouritism, then, have some basis in fact, if by that term we mean an essentially personalized selection for a few available vacancies. A further danger of this is the mistrust it breeds among the men themselves. Mainly because promotion competition was so keen, and so many of the men had so much to lose, there was a favourite axiom that 'you never trust anyone on this job'. Few, if any, of the men were prepared to express an opinion, let alone an adverse criticism, whilst one of their colleagues was present. This is in sharp contrast to the spirit in a large city force, where once a man has been duly tested and found 'all right' – an epithet endowed with great significance and meaning in this context – his colleagues of similar outlook on his shift, at least, and particularly his 'mate', will trust him implicitly.

The Royal Commission commented that in small forces promotion tends to stagnate, and it is harder than in a larger force for a chief constable to ignore the claims of seniority in filling the vacancies that occur. Many chief constables nowadays in fact try to alternate promotions between men with shorter and longer service, in order at the same time to encourage the keen younger men and to prevent the older men from wholly losing heart. Opposition to 'young' promotions is widespread in smaller forces, for the older men who have most influence on the general opinion see in this tendency their own chances waning. If the small force also happens to be a county one the position is worsened by the fact that men tend to retire later – the majority after 30 years' service as opposed to 25 years' in cities. Higher ranks are often tempted to stay on to their age limit, serving in all 35 years or more. There are two main reasons. One is that there are few if any jobs for untrained middle-aged men in such an area. The second is rooted in the housing problem already described, and the inability to commute the pension at less than 30 years' service. Those men serving for longer than 30 years tend to lose a certain amount of authority and prestige. To block promotion in this way is regarded, not always explicitly, as 'unsporting'.

Because of the promotion block almost all the men serving in small forces are in favour of amalgamation. They point out that what opposition to this there is comes from the top of the hierarchy, from chief constables, local authorities, and others afraid of the loss of status which might be involved. The lower ranks are all in favour. Although inter-force rivalry occurs, such feelings do not have to be reckoned with seriously; the basis is more than half humorous, and the advantages of combining are generally acknowledged. In small borough forces this is true also, although here the question is complicated by an additional anxiety. A man who has bought his own house in the borough will not be anxious to be posted to the county. He has a right to remain where he is throughout his service, yet he fears that if he elects to do so his own promotion chances will be cramped.

In view of this widespread feeling it is strange to find little mention of the advantages of amalgamation for promotion in the evidence given to the Royal Commission. The Association of Municipal Corporations considered the problem in relation to promotion, but said that it could be overcome by transfers between forces of the higher ranks. But such transfers, although desirable on other grounds, would not solve the problem already described of a promotion struggle at the constable-to-sergeant level. Only a larger operational unit could do this: perhaps the 'minimum optimum' of 500 arrived at by the Royal Commission should be taken as the standard. Now that the Home Secretary has increased powers in this respect we may hope for an improvement. As the Magistrates' Association said, 'From the point of view of a career there are obvious advantages in a national police force.' They at least realized the importance of morale in the sense that promotions should plainly lack bias. 'Forces should be large enough to provide scope for promotion and for obtaining experience of all branches of police work, they continued, 'while transfers between force in the higher ranks should be arranged.'

While the present proliferation of small forces continues there is one possible palliative. This is the institution of a promotion board. These render the selection of men for promotion more open and predictable. After qualifying, a candidate goes for interview before a board composed of the senior officers of his force. On the basis of these interviews a list is published of those constables who have passed both the qualifying examination and the board, that is those who can expect to be promoted. Qualified candidates not passed by the board may present themselves again for interview on an indefinite number of occasions, and it not infrequently happens that when a man has gained more practical experience the board will, on a subsequent occasion, pass him.

For the higher ranks competition for promotion is more widespread. It is for levels above that of inspector that inter-force transfers have been suggested. It is agreed that there would be too much opposition from the man in the 'host' force, especially from the qualified sergeants, if transfers became general on promotion to inspector. On the other hand, once such a system became fully operative antagonism of this kind would lessen. Host forces would tend to be large cities, where one or two 'immigrant' officers would quickly be absorbed in the total number.

Transfers later in service, although causing fewer problems of personal control, would give the 'immigrant' officers less opportunity to learn the 'on the ground' workings of their new forces, and leave them vulnerable to the ever-ready charge of being 'out of touch with real police work'.

So far the promotion question has been considered simply in terms of *whether* a suitably qualified candidate is likely to be promoted or not. Equally important from the point of view of attracting highly qualified recruits is *when* promotion is likely. In one force, the average length of service of a constable when 'made up' was 15·8 years, and no man at present serving as a sergeant had been promoted with less than 9 years' service. On average, these sergeants had held their rank for $5\frac{1}{2}$ years, and their mean length of service when the survey was carried out was 22 years. In this context it is understandable that throughout the force there should be antagonism to the institution of the new special course, designed specifically to facilitate speedy promotions for promising young men. The idea of a sergeant with only 5 or 6 years' service was automatically suspect: clearly he would be a 'book man'. More important, the danger was that they would block promotions for many years to come.

When the inspectors are considered the picture is even more startling. Their mean length of service was 28·6 years, and their average length of service on promotion 22·8. On average, 8 of these 23 years had been spent as sergeant; their mean length of service when first promoted being 14·9 years. Although this seems long enough for an able man to wait for a first promotion, it is a significantly shorter period than for those who were not subsequently made inspector (·05 level). In other words, the more capable men were in fact picked out for 'early' promotion in this force. It is unlikely that knowledge of such facts as these would encourage a high level of entry, and it must be emphasized that this force is not an extreme case.

The question is often asked whether police promotions are based on the number of convictions the candidates have to their name. The answer is no. In large urban forces the over-keen constable is unpopular with his colleagues, partly because he sets a standard for them which they do not wish to maintain, and partly because they too suffer if the public in their area are antagonized by his actions. Arrests and convictions are, however, required by the divisions to 'get the figures up' before the returns are sent in to headquarters and subsequently to the Home Office. C.I.D. men admitted that there was pressure to increase the proportion of crimes cleared up, but said that competition was between stations or sections rather than individual officers, as was once the case. When promotion in the C.I.D. was more difficult, they said, competition was more intense.

TRAINING

Training schemes are designed to offer in part solutions to both the recruitment and promotion difficulties, and with these aims in mind many of them are now nationally standardized.

Training of probationary constables in District Training Centres, of which there are eleven in the British Isles, concentrates mainly on police law and procedure, a large mass of information as yet unrelated to experience which must be digested or at least remembered. Recruits attend such a centre for three months after joining and subsequently for two fortnight-long refresher courses during their probation. Each course ends with an examination which the constable is required to pass, and a military style 'passing-out parade'. This system of training has not been re-examined for ten years. During that time related social sciences have developed considerably. Would it not be wise to incorporate some of the knowledge they contain into the recruits' training? Criminology and penology are obvious candidates for inclusion, but these alone are not enough. A rudimentary knowledge of social psychology could give the young policeman some insight into the nature of the problems with which he will have to deal, and, even more important, some understanding of the nature of his own reactions to these situations. Group discussions about the nature of the policeman's role and its relation to other social and welfare services could be of inestimable value, and help the recruit to build up a resistance to the antagonism he is bound to meet later from the older generation of police officers who may have lacked such training. Such discussions would doubtless be of value to longer service men also, as has already been found in the prison service.

A good pocket-size reference book on police law would obviate the need for much of the committing to memory of great chunks of indigestible material, and leave time on the course for the new subjects. The sight of recruits wandering, monk-like, round the grounds of the training centres intoning repeatedly the same passage from a legal textbook is not an edifying one. Policemen themselves maintain that 80 per cent of the information thus gained is of no further use to them, which is largely responsible for their assumption that all academic knowledge is as irrelevant as this. At the moment the recruit's main learning experience is his initial period on the beat with an older constable, who will instruct him in police lore and mythology, and indicate to him which opinions are most acceptable about matters relating to police work. Thus the evils in the system are at the moment perpetuated along with the good, for the recruit has no sound body of theory with which to counter this, but only a series of isolated and apparently irrelevant facts. Moreover, he is eager to be accepted by the group of serving officers, and therefore feels a strong need to conform to their ways of thought. Thus, though the senior officers may accept new ideas, the force as a body has a built-in resistance to them. Senior officers are powerless to counteract this for the acceptability of their own ideas is assessed by the men in terms of their general conformism to the conventional pattern.

So much for preliminary training. Also organized on a district or a force level are refresher courses for longer service constables, C.I.D. training courses, and all other types of specialist training. The men to attend these courses are selected by the chief constable on the recommendation of a senior officer, and he applies to the organizers of the course for a suitable number of vacancies. Men returning from specialist courses of all types tend to speak highly of their instructors and of the training they have received. It is in the teaching of general police work that the service falls short. All too often this shortcoming is excused by the claim that police work is something which it is impossible to teach anyway. There is an element of truth in this: a good policeman owes his success to some intangible element of personality; yet more suitable training could raise the level of both good and mediocre alike.

Centrally organized training schemes operate from the new Police College in Bramshill House, near Hartley Wintney in Hampshire – a magnificent country house standing in equally magnificent grounds, though the students live and work in the buildings put up since the Home Office took over. One of the most controversial schemes is the 'Special Course' for constables, which started in autumn 1962. The course is designed to provide a clear-cut avenue of promotion and career structure for able men with 'the potential to become future leaders', in the hope too that this first step towards rationalizing the promotion procedures will attract a higher proportion of well-qualified recruits. A constable puts his own name forward for selection, which takes place in three stages. A preliminary selection is based on the promotion examinations, places being divided proportionately on the basis of the number of candidates in the November and February sittings. A further sifting is carried out by a Central Selection Board, then a series of 'country house' interviews is held, and the final selection is made. Both staff and students of the college express great confidence in the interview procedure, which has been arrived at after an experimental year when candidates were also selected on the basis of their examination results alone. All are agreed that a future senior officer must have qualities additional to academic ability, and that the extended interview is the best-known means of assessing these. If the constable successfully completes this course he is promoted substantive sergeant immediately on returning to his force.

That the course has been regarded with a certain amount of suspicion within the service is understandable in view of the promotion opportunities previously described. In a small force one or two successful candidates on the course could effectively block promotion for older men for a year or more. As the course is of a year's duration older men do not feel inclined to attempt it, because it would mean leaving their homes for a prolonged period, as well as the additional effort needed to re-sit the promotion examination in order to qualify. The general attitude to 'book learning' also renders the course slightly suspect, and the Federation has admitted that it is watching its development closely. Bramshill must not smack too much of a second Hendon, which remains a dirty word with the vast majority of policemen.

There are four eleven-week terms for those on the Special Course, separated by two-week breaks; in addition there are two long weekends per term. Even so men from the extreme north and west complain with some justification that they cannot get home sufficiently often. Men from the Home Counties can make the journey most weekends, since they are free from Saturday evening until Monday morning. Compulsory sport on Saturday afternoons makes life more difficult for those who have further to travel, since this will usually involve entertaining the visiting team in the evening as well. Sport is also compulsory on Wednesday afternoons. The reasons given for this are that the job requires that the men should be physically fit. At Bramshill they are leading a far more sedentary life than usual, they have a lot of studying to do, and therefore they need to be 'made to get out'. As a secondary reason it was suggested that the contact with other establishments such as Sandhurst was useful, and that with so few men on the course volunteers alone would not provide adequate numbers to form the necessary teams. None of these reasons seems sufficient for treating adult men as juveniles. If these are the potential leaders of the future they must by definition be responsible people, who can surely be entrusted with responsibility for their own physical condition.

For the rest, the syllabus of the Special Course is admirable. Both police duties and general studies form part of the training in the first three terms; the fourth term is spent mainly in examinations and attachments to give the student an insight into the workings of forces of a different type from his own. In the first term the general studies course deals mainly with constitutional law and history. In the second it covers the field of the social sciences – politics, economics, and social studies. With so wide a syllabus the work lacks depth, but the attempt is a brave one, and the men appear to respond well. Social studies, for example, covers education, employment, social controls, land use, the welfare state and its effects, mass media, and, of course, the crime situation and the police in relation to society. Criminology, where this is touched upon, is dealt with as part of police studies concerned with criminal law. In the third term the general studies department concerns itself mainly with international affairs.

Such then is the first stage of training of those destined for high rank. The opportunity to exchange ideas and experience with officers from other forces and from abroad is valuable. Taken at face value the course itself is adequate; certainly it is a vast improvement on anything attempted hitherto. Yet where is it leading? The aims are described in vague terms such as 'broadening the mind' or 'developing leadership potential'. These express faith and hope in the ultimate outcome, but to plan a course successfully one's aims must be more coherent and specific. The more general results would follow automatically from a really good professional training. The college itself could help to develop a sound body of theory concerning the policeman's position, role, and function in various types of community, and far more attention should be paid to the accepted facts of social psychology so that the policeman can see his own behaviour and that of those with whom he has to deal both within and outside the force in a consistent theoretical framework. Instruction in a series of unrelated facts will never 'broaden the mind' in the sense of giving a broad perspective of perception and understanding.

There is less opportunity for men on the 'A' course to undergo instruction of this kind, since they are at the college for only six months. This is divided equally into a period of general studies and a period of police studies. The course is for sergeants, and is usually taken before promotion to inspector, though this is not necessary; and it also frequently happens that men are made substantive inspectors while still at Bramshill. Again the overall aim is 'to broaden the outlook'. One senior officer enlarged upon this by remarking that a man who had completed the course would 'know what to say to the mayor when sitting next to him at dinner'? To quote this is no doubt unfair. The majority have a far wider perspective, yet it is true that the police force as a whole suffers from a feeling of inferiority. They insist that officers should rise from the ranks yet are uncertain as to whether men who have done this could move on equal terms with high-ranking officers of the armed services. The truth is that there are so few occasions when they would have to, that the question itself is, although frequently asked, irrelevant.

Only 24 students attend the Senior Staff Course at one time, compared with maxima of 140 for the 'A' Course and 60 for the Special Course. Competition is, therefore, very keen. The course lasts for six months, and is in its first year of operation. It is 'designed to equip officers of the rank of inspector or above for the higher posts in the service'. A comprehensive report is made out on each student, as is also the case for other courses. From the ranks of those who have attended this course will be drawn the chief constables of the future.

These steps on the way to a rational, clearly visible, and consistent career structure will, it is hoped, attract better recruits in greater numbers. Why wastage is a more intractable problem is explained next.

CHAPTER 6

The Life of a Policeman
and his Family

This chapter examines the second aspect of the manpower situation, wastage, but fundamentally it is concerned with a far more basic question: what is a policeman's life like? For only when this question has been answered can it be understood why so many men leave the service before they are eligible to reap the benefits of their work.

The Association of Chief Police Officers has pointed out that almost half the wastage can be classed as 'abnormal' – not due to medical reasons or death, dismissal, or retirement with a long-service pension or gratuity. Before the announcement of the pay rise in November 1960, as can be seen from the graph on page 115, the wastage figures were consistently higher than those for recruitment. After this, the recruitment figures rose sharply and the wastage figures fell. But this gives a spurious picture. In the police service, pension is based on a man's average wage over the previous three years. A considerable number of men, therefore, who were eligible for retirement pension in terms of length of service but below the maximum age limit remained in the service for an additional two or three years to ensure that their pension was based on the new scale of pay. Since this scale became operative in September 1960, the effects of this averaging were not seen until September 1963. The last figure on the graph shows the change which took place when the period of averaging was over. Once again the number of men leaving the force is greater than the number joining. Since this exception in October, recruitment has again been greater than wastage, but in general it is significant that since Willink only 27 per cent of those leaving have retired on pension.

One of the most alarming aspects is the high proportion of long-service men who leave. True, the large bulk of wastage occurs during the first two years – $55\frac{1}{4}$ per cent of those who left between October 1962 and September 1963 did so in this period, although only 5 per cent of those leaving were probationary constables who had their services dispensed with. This wastage of probationary constables should not be classed as abnormal. These two years constitute a period of trial on both sides, and to leave during such a period is understandable. A policeman can resign at only a month's notice: there is little point in keeping unwilling or unsuited officers. One officer criticized the recruiting advertisements for leading men to expect that they could earn nearly £1,000 immediately. For those joining later in life than 19 or 20 years, the starting pay of £635 p.a. must entail considerable hardships, for a man who already has family commitments, despite free accommodation.

The remaining 45 per cent form the kernel of the problem. The men with more than 9 years' service formed 28·3 per cent of those leaving the force after the probationary period. Quite apart from the financial waste of the great cost of training a policeman, at whatever point of service he leaves, the loss of men with 9 years' service or more (those on maximum pay) has further disadvantages. These are the men who must be relied upon to teach the new recruits, the experienced men who can handle situations competently without calling for assistance from sergeants or senior officers, and men of the type who inspire confidence among members of the public. Because of their shortage recruits are not being given so thorough a groundwork in practical police duties, the beats are less adequately covered, and the public in large cities rarely sees the face of an older policeman unless they go to a station. The man behind the desk has great responsibilities and must be sound, which further starves the beat of its experienced men. This trend is emphasized in cities by the tendency for men to retire with 25 years' service, as opposed to the full 30 years which is more normal in the counties. But even in London 'the unsatisfactory strength of the force today is largely due to abnormal wastage', as the Commissioner stated in his 1962 Annual Report.

Among ex-Cadets wastage 'is only a small fraction of that in the case of direct entrants. It is possible during the comparatively long period of Cadet training to prepare a young man's mind in a way that will enable him to look intelligently at the task that lies before him, continued the Commissioner. This brings us closer to the heart of the matter: the reasons for leaving. Many have been suggested, but once again the morale factor has been almost totally ignored. Cadets know before they are sworn in what the job is about, and for this reason they are less likely to be disheartened by the drudgery of the first two years. Moreover, an ex-Cadet is only 19, so the low pay worries him less as he is unlikely to have family responsibilities. In addition, a Cadet tends to be educationally better qualified, so he may have higher ambitions for promotion which will ensure his remaining in the service.

The wastage rate is also affected by the 'pinpricks' factor, which is not usually mentioned by the man who leaves. More probably he would say that he was leaving for a job where the pay, hours, or conditions were better.

There are many examples of such pinpricks. One could be an unpopular senior officer. Another, frequently mentioned, is the feeling among older men that with increasing bureaucratization within the service their responsibility and freedom of movement is being sapped away. 'When I joined you'd deal with a case like this on your own, but nowadays you have to call the sergeant and before he'll do anything he has to contact the inspector – they're all afraid to move without asking the next one up today, and you can't get a decision from anyone without it going right back.' Another, less important, example of the sort of thing which can irritate men is the rule in one force that superintendents cannot give permission for the men to wear 'shirt sleeves'. This has to come from head-quarters, with the result that by the time the order comes through, the brief fine spell may well be over. There is another force which has a Standing Order to the effect that no repairs can be done to a police house without the superintendent's permission. The Order does not specify procedure in a case of emergency, so a man may find that due compensation for a legitimate repair is refused on the ground that no prior permission was given. Again, in one county force, the men were technically allowed to use their cars for an emergency, and a mileage allowance granted for this. But if a man had an urgent phone call to an accident, and on arrival in his car found that it was in fact only a minor bump – a circumstance which happens frequently – his claim for mileage would be refused on the

K

grounds that it was not an emergency, and that he would have arrived in plenty of time had he used his bicycle. Yet how was he to know the extent of the damage before he got there? There are frequent complaints about such retrospective logic on the part of superiors and innumerable further examples of pinprick factors. In sum, it can be said that they result from a desire to codify and regulate too rigidly, or carelessness and failure to explain a matter of policy, so that the men feel that their work is regarded as unimportant, and that scope for initiative or independent action is being drained from them.

Before the Royal Commission completed its report 41 per cent of the men leaving gave as their reason 'more pay'. In a survey carried out by the Federation in June 1963, only 47 of 1,750 men had complaints about this. 147 said they were leaving for some reason connected with the hours, and the remainder left either for 'domestic reasons' (525), or because of a generally expressed preference for other employment (768). The Federation suggests that these last two categories could well be bracketed together, as will be seen when the domestic tensions and problems resulting from police life are examined. Whatever the stated or unstated reason for leaving, there must also be some external pull before a man finally takes the plunge. This accounts for the difference in the wastage figures between large city forces and rural areas. In the former there are good alternative jobs to go to, better from the point of view of either pay or hours or both; in the country this is less often the case. Thus, although county men have as many, and perhaps more, causes for complaint, their rate of abnormal wastage is much lower.

PAY

The Federation claim that pay is no longer related to the wastage problem, although prior to 1960 it was definitely a major factor. Wastage declined soon after the announcement of the pay rise, and more than one man who had left rejoined subsequent to the pay increase. Men in a county force, where the relative position had never been so bad since country wages tend to be lower, said frequently that they had seriously considered leaving, but were prevented by the problem of finding a house. The low pay created the desire to leave but also forestalled it, since it made it impossible to save the necessary capital.

Over 85 per cent of those interviewed in 1963 said that they were at least 'fairly well satisfied' with the pay, though many added 'compared with what it used to be'. Those for whom the 'old days' provide the basis of comparison tend to be more satisfied than those who compare their pay with the current rates of workers in prospering local industries. The Willink Commission established the principle of a bi-annual review of police pay, and the first of these took place in September 1962.

In addition to the basic pay, accommodation is free and allowances are made for a number of extra expenses. These range from bicycle and boot allowances to detective duty and plain-clothes allowances. The income of a C.I.D. officer is usually roughly on a par with that of a man one rank higher in the uniformed branch, but his hours are longer, his general expenses greater, and his job more constantly taxing. However much overtime he may do, he is paid for only three hours, whereas his uniformed counterpart records his hours exactly and is paid accordingly. This leads to friction when uniformed men are

147

	commissioner	assistant commissioner	commander
Metropolitan Police	commissioner	assistant commissioner	commander
City of London Police	commissioner	assistant commissioner	—
other police forces	—	chief constable	—

	inspector	inspector (temporary)
Metropolitan Police	inspector	inspector (temporary)
City of London Police	inspector	—
other police forces	inspector	—

POLICE PAY: *Chief constables*

Provinces

Assistant chief constables	£2,160–£3,050
Chief constables	£1,735–£5,355

Metropolitan

Deputy commander	£3,820–£3,050
Commander	£3,390–£3,780
Assistant commissioner	£4,840
Deputy commissioner	£5,355

deputy commander	chief superintendent	superintendent (grade 1)	superintendent (grade II)	chief inspector
—	chief superintendent	superintendent (grado 1)	superintendent (grade II)	chief inspector
assist. chief constable		chief superintendent	superintendent (grades I & II)	chief inspector

station sergeant	sergeant	acting sergeant
—	sergeant	acting sergeant
—	sergeant	acting sergeant

POLICE PAY: *Ranks up to and including chief superintendent*

Constable	£ 635–£1,030
Sergeant	£1,090–£1,170
Station sergeant (Metropolitan police only)	£1,215–£1,255
Inspector	£1,280–£1,370
Chief inspector	£1,435–£1,530
Superintendent	£1,700–£2,005
Chief superintendent	£2,040–£2,160

Note Metropolitan and City of London constables and sergeants also receive £20 p.a. London allowance.

'loaned' to the C.I.D. for the duration of a particular inquiry and the difference becomes apparent. As long ago as 1947 the Federation asked that detective duty allowance should be based on six hours. Some officers would prefer that the job was fully salaried and payment for overtime abolished.

HOURS

The Federation is convinced that the root of the manpower problem lies in the uncongenial hours of duty, and it is making every possible effort to reduce these. Until July 1964 a policeman works an 88-hour fortnight, with two rest days in one week and one in the week following. This is the theory; in practice several large forces have found it impossible to grant their men more than one day's leave a week, and they receive pay in compensation for the additional day a fortnight worked, although since the pay rise the men themselves say they would prefer extra leave to extra pay. A vicious circle is thus established. The long hours induce men to leave and increase the shortage, meaning that those who remain have to work longer hours, which in turn has the same effect of reducing manpower.

But it is not only the number of hours worked which is a cause for complaint; in themselves these are not unreasonable. But police work has to continue throughout 24 hours a day. The peak hours of activity are in the evening and early hours of the morning. This means that the men must work shifts. More men would mean greater flexibility. Some forces still adhere to the old three-shift system – 6 a.m. to 2 p.m., 2 p.m. to 10 p.m., and 10 p.m. to 6 a.m. As both the men concerned and their wives point out, this means that they never have a 'normal' working day. On 'first watch' they must get up at 4.30 a.m. or 5 a.m. to be at the police station to parade at 5.45 a.m. Thus although the afternoon and evening are technically free the man will be too tired to want a great deal of social activity. The afternoon shift effectively renders such activity impossible, and the night shift does too, since the man must be at the police station by 9.45 p.m. Wives too are therefore often unable to live a normal family life.

A better variant of this is the five-shift system worked by the Metropolitan Police and others. Here there are two additional, overlapping shifts, one from 9 a.m. to 5 p.m., which corresponds with a normal working day, and another from 5 p.m. to 1 a.m. which is less popular, but covers the peak period for police work. London's traffic problem means that more men are required during the day, and although traffic duties tend to be unpopular, the hours of duty they entail are a great advantage to the men.

There are, however, a number of policemen who claim that they prefer shift work, and that they would find regular office hours intolerable. These are mainly men with young, pre-school-age families. For them, a leave day in the week is an advantage, since there is less traffic if they wish to travel, and more activity locally if not. Others claim that on shift work they see more of their children than other men do, since they are home during the day when the children are up and about. They can also act as baby-sitters while their wives do the shopping and help in many other ways.

The problems come to a head, however, when the children start school. After then they very rarely see their father, who is working or sleeping much of the time when they are at home. Nor does he see them on his leave day, except on the one occasion in seven when it falls at a weekend. It is small wonder that family friction develops. Many wives speak of how they and their children watch neighbouring families going out together on Sundays and Bank Holidays, and wish that they could do the same.

There are further snags with children of school age when it comes to annual leave. In a large force it is plain that not all the men can have their leave during the limited period of the school holidays, yet a leave when the children are at school means that the family cannot go away together. Often the wife will take the children away and the husband join them on his leave day if possible, or they may arrange their holiday to coincide with one of the rare long weekends which occur when leave for two weeks falls together between the right shifts. But even three days in a fortnight is unsatisfactory from the family's point of view, and a cause of justifiable complaint. Too few recruits realize these disadvantages when they join.

Nor is shift work a problem only when the men have children. Before that, if they are married and their wife is at work, there is the difficulty that they rarely see each other. She may be working normal office hours with the weekend free, so often they will see each other only *en passant* as one goes to work and the other returns. Men who have married policewomen say that theirs is the only work to combine with their own from the point of view of hours: the man and his wife can arrange to be on the same leave code so that their days off coincide.

In a county force a whole different set of difficulties applies. A man in a country beat station is on call for 24 hours a day, although he may officially have set hours of duty. There are advantages in this, in that he can arrange his hours, if these are left to his own discretion, to suit his personal convenience, so long as this does not interfere with the job. The disadvantage is the uncertainty; both the men and their wives find that after a time this tells on them, because they are never able to make a definite arrangement, but always have to say 'providing nothing happens'. All too often something does happen to upset domestic plans during hours off, and even worse, on leave days when the family had arranged to go out. Nor can anything be done to stop local callers from coming with their problems in off-duty hours. If they see their policeman at home they assume that he is on duty, and he cannot very well send them away when they may live at some distance. Such comments as the following are common. 'If I want to get away from work on my rest day I have to go out. That means I can't just enjoy my home in the normal way and relax there. All the time, whether you've done your eight hours or not, there's people coming to the door and they expect you to be at home.' Understandably, the wives and families and the men themselves find this perpetual invasion of their privacy a source of great tension.

Even when her husband is out, the country policeman's wife is tied to the job. She must take phone messages and attend to callers while her husband is out on the beat, and often does so even when he is off-duty. The work of a country policeman should not be measured in terms of incidents dealt with or hours spent on the beat, but rather in terms of general wear and tear and responsibility.

FAMILY PROBLEMS

Tensions rooted in the inter-relationships between the policeman, his family, the community in which he lives, and his colleagues and superiors affect the town and country forces differently. A study carried out in 1962 and early 1963 showed that tension between the husband and wife was very slightly greater in the county force, as were tensions generated by the relationship between the policeman and the local community. Similar conflicts between the men and their colleagues or superiors were far more frequent in the county. In one experimental situation 73·4 per cent of the men said they would experience these, compared with 54·5 per cent of those in the city.

Family tensions are perhaps the most important factor in wastage, though their overall incidence was lower than that for conflicts arising from the other sources.

> A police constable does not merely take a job; he embarks on a new way of life . . . the first claim on him must be made by his duty and the convenience of his wife and family must be a secondary consideration.[1]

This applies not only to constables. One superintendent told how his annual leave had been postponed by the chief constable just as he and his wife had their bags packed and were on the point of leaving the house. Such incidents occur more frequently in county forces, where the hierarchy of authority remains more autocratic. Yet despite this, country policemen's wives frequently say 'Oh, one gets to accept it. It's all part of the job.' Because of this attitude many of the potential conflicts inherent in their situation never became actual: 59 per cent of the country policemen said they were satisfied with the effects of the job on their private life, compared with 51 per cent of the city men.

[1] Association of Chief Police Officers in evidence to the Royal Commission on the Police. Minutes of Evidence 4 (Part 11), p. 260.

These proportions are, however, low even in the county force. The hours and the inability to make arrangements are the main causes of dissatisfaction, but there are others as well. In the county the greatest inconvenience to the family is caused by frequency of transfer. In one force the men's average length of stay in a post was 2·7 years – just sufficient time for the whole family to form roots so that the next move would again entail an emotional as well as a physical upheaval. Adults can adapt themselves to this situation; at least they are able to choose; children cannot. Eldest children of the county men averaged four schools each; over a quarter of the children had already attended five schools or more. Here are some of the men's own comments about this: 'The elder girl suffered from this last move. She had to give up taking one or two subjects which weren't taught at the new school.'

'All this changing schools is the trouble with a county force. There was my girl of eight, she could hardly read. And when this business of the eleven plus came along for the elder one I realized for the first time what I'd been doing to my children.'

Another man told of how he had been obliged to move on the day before his daughter sat for her eleven-plus, and others of how their children had been emotionally disturbed for months after a particularly inopportune move. In the county 69 per cent of the children were said to have an unfavourable opinion of their father's job, compared with 35 per cent in the city. 18 per cent of policemen who were interviewed in one force said that they would not wish any eligible son of theirs to join the police.

Only a few of the parents said that their children met with antagonism because of their father's work, but there were rather more in the country than in the towns, where school-fellows do not necessarily know his occupation. Again, in the country, more men said that their children suffered because teachers and others in authority expected a higher standard or 'example' from them.

From the wife's point of view the moves entail far more than the loss of friends. There is the additional work and expense of refitting curtains and carpets every three years, and the redecoration of the new house. The maximum allowance of £30 goes only a small way towards meeting these expenses. There is therefore no incentive to plant the garden or decorate the house, though in fairness it must be said that most stations are very well kept. On average the wives had each lived in four police houses. In some forces, bad administration causes families to be given only a fortnight's notice or less before a move.

A higher standard is expected of the policeman's family in such matters, and they are all very much aware of this. Physically isolated and lacking the support of their colleagues, known personally to all the local inhabitants, the country policeman is highly vulnerable to criticism from his neighbours. For this reason he attempts to conform to their expectations of him, and he experiences conflict when he is unable to do so. The city man can get encouragement from his colleagues should such a situation arise. He is also in a stronger position in that he is often uncertain of what the general public really expects him to do, and if he does know he may be indifferent since he need not come into contact with those who disagree. Avoidance is the simplest way of resolving such a potential conflict. Speaking of a minor motoring offence which might occur at an inconvenient time, one country beat man said, 'If it were on my own patch I'd have to do something, because people would see and wonder if I let him off; you can't afford to do that. But if it happened somewhere else, well, then that would be different.' Another remarked, 'I always try to look as a policeman should be dressed . . . In a little town like this it would be very difficult for anyone who liked to dress casually. One thing, you see, everyone knows you. . . .'

A myth has grown up among city folk that the country policeman has an idyllic life as the hub and centre of his own little world, a man treated with respect and courtesy by the local people, and whose judgement is relied upon implicitly in a wide variety of matters. Much of this is true, but there are other equally important factors left out of the description. The life of a county policeman in a rural area can be a very lonely one. It is true that he is treated with respect, but this by definition implies a certain amount of social distance. All too often he is regarded as someone 'different', with whom it would therefore be impossible to make friends on equal terms, and his wife and family also will be treated with a not unkindly meant wariness: 'I think they like me all right but they're not friendly,' said one country policeman's wife. Isolation based on respect is as painful as isolation based on mistrust. Another rural wife spoke of her embarrassment when the local shopkeeper regularly insisted on serving her first, regardless of how many other customers were already waiting; while many more said that conversation tended to stop when they approached.

INTEGRATION OR ISOLATION?

How far in fact are policemen a race apart? And how far does such separateness as does exist result from their own choosing? Broadly speaking, city police either do not come into contact with civilians to any great extent because they live in a group of police houses, or because they have chosen to be isolated. In the country the contact is there. More often than not the isolation is forced on the policeman's family by the local population, though here too there are those who choose it. 'If you get too friendly and they do something wrong they expect you either not to report them or to cover it up in such a way that they're not prosecuted.' This is not always the case. In an organically solid village community the consensus of values is high. One constable spoke of an occasion when a personal friend continued to infringe the Diseases of Animals Regulations, after repeated warnings. With apologies the constable explained that he would now have to report him, but that he hoped their relationship would remain friendly. Apparently it did. A policeman is expected to do his job. But the fact that this compromise solution worked in this case does not mean that the conflict the constable experienced was any the less, and it is understandable that many men choose instead to avoid friendship and therefore potential conflict. As the Federation representatives have said, a policeman 'cannot expect to enjoy full social freedom in the police district where he serves', and if a man happens to live in the district where he serves, that is a misfortune. His behaviour must always be exemplary, as must that of his family, and his duty as a policeman must always be uppermost in his mind, for those with whom he comes into contact will regard him primarily as a policeman and will force professional considerations upon him although technically he may be off duty and more anxious to turn his mind to leisure pursuits. Such is the strain under which the rural constable often lives, not from choice and not because his senior officers demand it from him, but because the people on his beat expect it of him. He must conform because both he and his family are dependent upon their good will and co-operation.

The expectations of the community will vary from place to place, and they will certainly differ at many points from the expectations of the higher ranks of the force. The community will have its own ideas as to which offences should be dealt with severely and which should not, how often a policeman should visit and how he should behave when he does. City-born men working country beats often spoke of the length of time it took them to settle down, in particular to adjust their pace of working to that of the people they were dealing with. These community opinions carry heavy sanctions, and strong conflicts can arise for the man whose family or superiors have a different set of expectations about his behaviour.

Just how much contact do the policeman and his family have with the wider community? Despite difficulties of transport and physical isolation the men in the county force met more civilians socially on more occasions than did the city men. The total scaled score for social contact with the community was 3·3 on average for the county men, and 2·4 for those in the city. This bears out the hypothesis of the county man being more dependent on the local civilan population. But his desire to be accepted by this civilian community is also stronger on account of this greater dependence, and 74 per cent of the county men compared with 44 per cent of the city men thought that they would have more friends if they had a different job. (The Royal Commission Survey found that 66·8 per cent of policemen said that the job adversely affected their outside friendships.) City men tended to show a cheerful confidence about their social relationships with the community at large, since these relationships were less important for them, and they claimed to have more friends locally than did the men from the rural areas. Yet only 40 per cent of the city men had been born in the same town or county, compared with 64 per cent of the men from the county force.

For the wives the relationship between the two forces was rather different. 59 per cent of the county wives and 55 per cent of the city wives had been born locally. The county wives met fewer people socially than did their husbands, but they tended to see these few people more frequently. Wives in the city met more people socially than did their husbands, as well as seeing them more often, and they also scored much more than the country wives on both these counts. It is understandable that the wife of a country policeman becomes dissatisfied when her social life is so much restricted. Physical distance and the demands of the job mean that she can leave home less often, so she even tends to see her relatives less often than her husband or the city women did. At the same time she lacks her husband's opportunity for meeting many people each day on a professional level. Country wives were also more isolated than their equivalents in the city in their contacts with the families of other policemen. One reason for this is that 17 per cent of the county wives compared with 25 per cent of the city wives lived in groups of six or more police houses. Moreover, there were fewer organized social activities for wives and families in the county, as well as the ever-present problem of poor public transport and physical distance.

For the men in rural areas it would seem that transport

is not a worry. Just as they had a greater number of social contacts with civilians than did their city counterparts, so too they had on average social contacts with more fellow policemen. These contacts were mainly at sporting activities organized by the force, whereas in the city they tended to be less formal. For the city men too their work each day involved contact with their colleagues. This accounts for the fact that the county men claimed far more often than city men that their colleagues or superiors would disagree with an action they intended to take. In a conflict situation it is far more important to them that they should conform to the expectations of their family, or their local community, than with their colleagues or superiors whom they see far less frequently and who are unlikely to watch what they do.

For the city man the situation is quite different. Often he will work some distance from home so his family and neighbours need not know of his actions at work, whereas he is in frequent contact with his fellow policemen, and dependent on their backing. He must therefore conform to their expectations and not forfeit their goodwill. Thus the city man will tend to solve his conflicts or conflicting expectations in accordance with the requirements of his fellow policemen.

Although there are no corresponding figures for the total community with which to compare them, the available data suggest that the relative isolation of both the men and their wives that policemen often talk of is not in many cases fact, although it is both perceived and experienced. This perception and the tensions resulting from the conflict experiences which have been described (especially in the country where the man's actions are visible to at least two of the groups concerned) and the strain of being constantly in the public gaze are all factors in wastage. The fact is that quite apart from professional work, a large number of actions which would normally be private are controlled to some extent by the expectations of work-mates, superiors, and the public at large.

RELATIONSHIPS INSIDE THE FORCE

These varied again between the city and the county. The city men claimed to have more friends on the job – statistically, 5·3 as against 3·1 in the county. County men said that those friends they had were men with whom they had joined. It was not always wise to get too friendly with men working neighbouring beats: they were suspicious of their colleagues because of the promotion struggle and because of the fear that if a mistake is made and discovered a sudden transfer could result. In any case, the men say that firm friendships are impossible when one is constantly being moved. In the city the picture is different. Friend-ships tend to develop in working together on the beat or mobile patrol, in sharing difficulties over some disruly members of the public or over a senior officer. The backing of colleagues is essential in a tight corner and strong ties of loyalty develop. This loyalty is the prime virtue, together with the other 'heroic' attitude that the weak must be protected: wives and such women as could be regarded as potential wives are treated with exaggerated respect (which involves leaving them in considerable ignorance of many of their menfolk's activities). This last attitude also enables them to avoid conflict between some of the demands of their job and their family's expectations for them. It was significant that on an inter-dependence scale the city men scored much higher than those in the county

(4·7 compared with 2·6). They perceived both themselves to be far more dependent on the force, and the force to be far more dependent on them, than did the county men.

There are some points at which the relationships with other members of the force can lead to wastage. In city forces much of the formality has been dropped from these relationships between ranks, but in the county the hierarchic structure is rigidly adhered to. A county inspector would never call one of his constables by his christian name while on duty, and it is unlikely that he would do so off duty either. The relationship with senior officers in the county remains to some extent paternalistic. Thus fewer men said they were dissatisfied with the amount of interest their superiors took in them than of the city men. Yet senior officers in the county are more feared, for they have correspondingly more autocratic powers. Their authority under the Discipline and other regulations is the same in both forces, but in the county infringements tend to be arbitrarily 'punished' by a transfer, without formal examination. If a query should arise the move can always be justified on other grounds. So a county man is anxious always to 'keep in step' with his superiors, because otherwise his whole family will suffer. In the city discipline matters are dealt with more openly, and generally the Federation is strong enough to see fair play.

The rationalization of discipline in the larger forces, whether city or county, is a further example of that process of increasing bureaucratization which is itself causing tensions of a different kind at other points. One is that the beat men feel that their individual responsibility is being sapped away and that their job is therefore a less interesting one, and this is true in many cases. Further tensions of bureaucratization arise where the structure is not yet completely rational. Men in specialist departments, such as dog handlers and mobile patrols, often claim that they are the victims of divided authorities which on occasion can give conflicting orders. They are responsible both to their specialist superiors and to the senior officers of the divisions where they work. 'You've always got one of them on your back, and it makes things very difficult. You can't please everyone.' Although legally he alone is responsible for his actions and must bear the consequences of them, the constable is in the anomalous position that he also has the opinions of his senior officers to bear in mind. He has to satisfy their requirements, those of the people with whom he is dealing, and the law. In the city these responsibilities will be considered in that order; in the country the first two may well be reversed.

THE POLICE AS A MINORITY GROUP

As members of what is by definition a minority group, the police are continuously in a defensive position. Their uniform is a visible cue for prejudice against them, and they become sensitive and unable to concede the need for any internal change as a result. Some of them lessen the tension produced by this situation by attempting to disown the job, and conform as far as possible to more general standards. 'I always go home in civvies; you don't want to advertise the fact that you're a copper, do you?' 72 per cent of men interviewed said they did not like to be recognized as policemen while on holiday. Others attempt to exclude themselves from what they perceive to be a general public attitude of antagonism by saying that the force has changed since they joined, that young men joining today are of a lower standard, and that the job is not the same any more. (Even some young men do this.) Those who have done National Service say that the trouble lies with those who haven't; those who enter direct say that the trouble lies with the increased numbers of cadets. Much of this dissatisfaction results from a feeling of low status, which in turn sometimes gives rise to violence, verbal or physical, against prisoners as an outlet, which gives further backing to the negative stereotype. In parts this accounts for the greater incidence of violence in city areas, where the public expectations are less favourable. The realization of this is one of the causes of early leaving, though it is unlikely to appear in statistics of reasons for leaving, since the men concerned are scarcely aware of it on a conscious level.

HOUSING

Accommodation in 'police colonies' can serve only to enhance this feeling of separateness. In the main the men do not want to admit that they are different (though in fact they are more conscious of the difference than most members of the public), and housing of this type is never popular. The wives as well object to living in too close proximity with other police wives. There are problems of rank, embarrassments when friends get promoted, which the wives feel more keenly than the men since they have no accepted pattern of behaviour to follow in this situation. There are problems too of lack of privacy: the feeling of being constantly under the gaze of neighbours leads to friction. The men bring their work problems home, and the atmosphere can deteriorate into one of unkind gossip and antagonisms. Another problem arises between women whose husbands work different hours. One may be in the C.I.D., and another on shift work. Each will regard the lot of the other as the more favourable, probably because the one does not have to work night duties, while the other can always plan his free time in advance.

Significantly only 18 per cent of the men in one force stated categorically that they would prefer to live with other policemen, and most of these objected to the large colonies. Yet though large police colonies are unpopular, the men do not want to live with the general public indiscriminately. There are frequent complaints about police houses or flats in 'bad areas', about the schools in these areas which the children have to attend, and the lack of 'suitable' playmates for them. This applies to the adults too. One wife remarked, 'I mean, you couldn't make friends with the people round here, could you?' and another, for the same reason, 'I don't see many civvies really; you wouldn't make friends in an area like this anyway.' Yet local authorities cannot give their police preference in the siting of houses: their situation is a matter of expediency, rather than a result of any established policy that the men should 'mix'. The colonies are too the result of purely practical considerations. In the past it was cheaper and easier to build large numbers of houses together, but the dangers of this practice in minority group feelings and tensions inside the force have now been recognized, and very few police authorities would now build more than ten houses in a cluster. But it will be many years before this particular source of wastage can be removed.

CONCLUSION

These, then, are the main reasons for early leaving. Many of them, as has been seen, stem from the fact that the tasks determined for the policeman by society do not conform to either his own or the public's conception of his role, and they also impinge on his role in family life. Yet none of these factors independently is sufficient cause for a man to leave; their effect is cumulative. Again it must be emphasized that the 'pull' factor, the external circumstance which seems so much better than one's own, must be present before a man will leave. This accounts for the much greater loss of manpower in the urban areas, although the tensions produced by the job in a rural area are equally great. Many of them are everywhere unavoidable; others could be reduced if some senior officers had a greater insight into the nature of the problems with which their men have to cope. A long look at their own relationships both with colleagues and the men under their command might help. Police training should now be geared to the reduction of the service's most pressing problem: both senior officers and men should be shown how to make an objective appraisal of their position in society and thus helped to adjust to it and each other.

CHAPTER 7

Quis Custodiet?

COMPLAINTS AGAINST THE POLICE

Most of us are eager to enjoy the pleasurable satisfaction of hearing complaints against those in authority. A ready audience can always be found for allegations against cabinet ministers, schoolmasters, clergy, royalty, and, above all, the police. The result is a curious reversal of normal liberal values. Otherwise fair-minded people have an indefensible tendency to assume the guilt of the police until they are proved innocent, and sometimes even after. Some of those who were loudest in condemning Senator McCarthy for his technique of guilt-by-association are often the same people who habitually smear 'the police' with the failings of one or two officers. In incidents which involve allegations against policemen, people seem to be carried by their emotions into an inhumanity that they would denounce as unjust and sadistic on other occasions.

Because the exoneration of an innocent policeman rarely seems to give them comparable pleasure, the actual number of allegations that are well founded must be a disappointment to some of these illiberals. Of the 1,722 complaints made against the Metropolitan Police in 1962, 10 per cent were substantiated. What is less widely known is that the Worcestershire police, for example, get twenty-one letters of appreciation for every two of complaint that they receive. But because any attempt to cover up an incident will destroy the public's faith in the police, and because one defaulting policeman who is unchecked can lose goodwill for the whole force, it is vital for the police themselves that every allegation is cleared up satisfactorily. A special commission should have offered to follow up each of the cases of complaint revealed in the Social Survey. The number of staff who investigate complaints ought to be augmented as a matter of priority. Even if the 'rubber-heeled squad' is the least wanted job in the service, their preventive effect within the police force is as vital as the necessity to identify a defaulter at the earliest possible moment.

It is because the present arrangements for handling complaints do not satisfy the public that many have to be investigated by, for example, the National Council for Civil Liberties,[1] who receive about 300 complaints against the police each year (of which they estimate some 50 appear to be well founded, and 10 substantiable). The overworked volunteers at the N.C.C.L. (who also take up cases on behalf of individual policemen) are doing work which should really be done by an Ombudsman. It is regrettable that some senior police officers show a hostile attitude to the N.C.C.L.: they refused, for example, on one occasion to show the Council a specimen police warrant-card – although it is in the public interest that people should be able to identify bogus policemen. Police officers are wrong to sneer at the N.C.C.L., who are performing a valuable function: in Athens, some people once grew tired of Socrates. The N.C.C.L. and the police are at heart pursuing identical objects: they should form a permanent joint committee and work together.

Research should have been undertaken a long time ago

[1] 4, Camden High St, NW1.

into the aetiology of complaints against the police. Although it is difficult for the individual policeman not to feel personally aggrieved when his career is threatened by a complaint, some criminals are only attacking the police as symbols of the society which they think has treated them badly. A few criminals have been known to plant complaints so as to preoccupy a particular detective officer who is following them too closely. Some originate from neurotic people who develop a deluded fixation that they are being persecuted by the police, who are the most accessible personifications of Fate. Others come from touchy people whose *amour propre* is hurt if they are spoken to by anyone in authority. Some are justified: the police, like most human beings, often reciprocate the attitudes and behaviour of the people they are dealing with. In addition, they may be under other pressures: the need to improve on their predecessor's figures in a situation which is continually worsening; or a sense of loyalty to a colleague; or perhaps the attempt to justify some wrong procedure adopted in the confusion of an arrest.

Whatever their origin or foundation, it is essential for the police themselves that complaints against them are investigated as speedily as possible. When, for example, it was widely reported by newspapers in June 1963 that a prisoner in Edinburgh alleged that he had had both his arms broken by police taking his fingerprints, irreparable damage was caused by the seven days' delay before it was announced that doctors said he had no recent fracture to either arm. In case after case recently, Lord Trenchard's maxim for police public relations 'Tell the truth – immediately' appears to have been forgotten.

One chief constable said: 'Perhaps the real trouble lies in some chief constables being unable to admit mistakes by their men gracefully.' A determined member of the public recently described[1] how he had to spend £200 before he was able to wring even an apology out of the Metropolitan Police. Another chief constable said that after Sheffield some police officers were almost neurotic about criticism, and that they tended to see in newspapers only allegations directed against them. The C.I.D. of one city force in 1962 went so far as unofficially to work to rule because they felt they were not getting backing-up from their chief constable against the public, when he disciplined two of their number. (In cases when their support is justified, Police Authorities should act much more quickly in giving it: considerable damage to morale in the past has resulted from delay in, for example, refunding damages or costs inadvertently incurred by an officer in his duties.)

But contrary to what many policemen think, it is not the reports of police misconduct which worry the public. The Social Survey, which was taken soon after Brighton, Worcester, and Thurso, showed that most members of the public had great faith in the police and must have been aware that these cases were the actions of individual human beings who happened to be policemen. The prosecution of a guilty policeman in fact renews the public's confidence and thankfulness that they live in one of the countries where this happens (instead of, for instance, in Spain, where those who protested about police misconduct in 1963 were charged with military rebellion). But what was even more serious than the violence at Sheffield in 1963 was the disclosure, in the subsequent Inquiry's Report, of wholesale cover-up and even fabrication of evidence by several police officers. The violence is unanimously condemned by the police themselves ('absolutely

[1] In *The Police and the Public*, ed. by C. H. Rolph.

disgraceful and disgusting,' said the Secretary of the Police Federation); but the glimpse the Inquiry gave of the police's investigation of that case made everybody in the country, with the apparent exception of the Home Secretary, realize that independent inquiries are thereafter inevitable. Most chief constables investigate scrupulously (and not by means of the very officers involved, as happened at Sheffield), but this incident marks a turning point, after which the public will be satisfied only by the presence of someone from outside the police at the inquiries. The present system not only breeds rumours, but also weakens the value of police evidence on other questions—which is a serious matter for a legal system which is dependent on juries.

The other grave revelation made by the incident at Sheffield was that, although (as at Brighton between 1951 and 1958) many officers must have known the truth, not one member of either of these forces had the integrity to come forward and speak out. The trouble is that the wrong loyalties are, at times, uppermost and strongest in the police today: comrades and the service come first, with justice and the public a poor second. (How can these men be surprised that the public do not help them more?) As they feel their authority decline, internal solidarity has become increasingly important to the police. Despite the individual responsibility of each police officer to pursue justice, there is sometimes a tendency to close ranks and to form a square when they themselves are concerned. At the trial of a Glasgow constable acquitted of the culpable homicide of a prisoner in November 1963, one of his colleagues admitted that he kept the facts relating to the man's death back from the investigating officers, and the Judge said of a third constable, 'He could not hear, or speak, or see any evil.' The majority of policemen, however, now realize that an attempt to whitewash invariably does more harm than good in the long run. Most of them, including some chief constables, realize that independent inquiries will be to their own advantage, and are anxious for them: 52 per cent of the officers who were questioned in 1963 said that they were in favour of inquiries into all serious allegations against the police being conducted by an independent chairman, such as a lawyer.

The police make it harder for people to appreciate the true incidence of misconduct by not publishing full details of complaints. Some idea can be gained from the numbers, out of the 58,000 policemen in the forces outside London in England and Wales, who have been required to resign or have been dismissed on being convicted of a criminal offence:

1956 : 24	1960 : 31
1957 : 20	1961 : 25
1958 : 23	1962 : 33
1959 : 45	

The standard of police conduct is usually set by the senior officer at each police station, in the same way as a chief officer does in each prison. Lawyers find that allegations are almost invariably made against the same minority of police officers, who frequently come from the same few stations. Some solicitors have built up their own record files of descriptions of these detectives: they form not more than 5 per cent of the C.I.D., but are among its most active officers. (The bulk of complaints have always been made against the C.I.D.: this may be because, whether or not the uniformed branch are citizens in uniform, C.I.D. officers are policemen out of uniform.)

Complaints against the police fall into three main categories: corruption, perjury, or violence. This book is not the place in which to investigate new cases: trial should not be by print. The incidents which are recounted in this chapter in order to illustrate the problems and points of friction of the public have all been either related by police officers themselves or are well substantiated. The reader should bear in mind that they refer to only a small proportion of an enormous force of human beings – perhaps no greater a proportion than there are of similar people amongst lawyers, M.P.s, journalists, and the other most frequent critics of the police.

CORRUPTION

SECOND WATCHMAN:		If we know him to be a thief, shall we not lay hands on him?
DOGBERRY	[a constable]:	Truly, by your office, you may; but I think they that touch pitch will be defiled.

(*Much Ado About Nothing*, Act 3, Scene 3)

A good C.I.D. officer lives a great deal among the criminal world, sharing both its haunts and its thoughts as he and the professional criminal try to read each other's minds.[1] Temptation probably comes more frequently in his work than anybody else in society. We demand that a good detective will be adept at bribing and blackmailing informers on our behalf, but never on his own. He often knows as well that the man who tries to bribe him has no

[1] Though not all criminals' talk of the mutual acceptance they and policemen have for each other should be believed: it adds to their status to say that they have a 'working relationship' with the police.

moral right to the money he is offering. The opportunities are so great that the police are expected to be above suspicion: there are Draconian penalties for any default (though the maximum penalty for theft by a police officer is not so high as it is for a postman). Rapid transfer of officers to a new area have to be balanced against the social dislocation and the loss of information and contacts which this causes. A C.I.D. officer has a unique free-lance relationship of mutual trust with his circle of informers.[1] These are the men who are responsible for the gap of 'information received' which is never disclosed at trials, and generally they are ex-criminals who have reached the criminal menopause. A few are still active themselves, and open their mouths either because the criminal world (like the legal one) likes talking shop, or else out of motives of envy or spite, or in order to escape their own deserts. Payments are small: often just the price of a drink or two, rarely £25 or at most £50, and always paid after the information is proved correct. But now that insurance assessors are giving 10 per cent of the value of stolen goods for their recovery without an arrest, informers have a more profitable trade, and sometimes are able to earn £5,000 a year. The protection given to informers, unless it is carefully watched, could become a vested interest which causes a net loss to the community.

The bulk of police dishonesty has always occured in connexion with those offences which public opinion does not regard as morally reprehensible, and which the police have a wide discretion in prosecuting, such as the sale of obscene books. (The two largest classes of client, street bookmakers and street prostitutes, are now ended.) This confinement to the fringes of crime is different from the

[1] Known as 'grasses', 'narks', 'fingers', 'snouts', or 'squeakers'.

position in the United States, where, for example, in 1961 some fifty Denver policemen were found to have been operating a professional crime syndicate using police cars for the previous ten years.

Experienced officers and criminal lawyers say that police corruption in this country is minimal, and has decreased since before the Second World War. It is unlikely to be cured by raising pay, which is now fairly adequate: although professional crime has now become so profitable and organized that three- and four-figure bribes can be offered, police officers say that corruption remains rare and on a much more petty scale. A few garages, for example, pay policemen for recommending the drivers of broken-down cars; some street-traders buy toleration; a Special in the East End of London said gifts tended to take the form of kippers or fruit. A number of motorists have a story of the successful deployment of a pound note wrapped round their driving licence (often it is those who are proud of having done the bribing who make allegations of corruption). One sergeant who used to be on duty in Soho said that his income dropped appreciably when he moved, and also had previously been reduced when an obscene post-card seller began to have to pay his £20 a month to the Vice Squad.

It is the custom of a few police officers, when they are the first to arrive at the scene of a shopbreaking, to pick a few things for themselves. The professional criminal 'Robert Allerton' stated in *The Courage of his Convictions* that he had bought his way out of more charges than those he had been to prison for. But the most commonly reported source of illicit police earning is from defendants who 'put in the bung' in order to gain favourable evidence at their trial on ancillary matters, such as their previous record and co-operation (which may affect their sentence but not their conviction).[1]

It is not asking too much that this should be totally suppressed. No probation officer, who receives less pay than many policemen, has ever been known to take money although he has the same opportunities. It is no excuse for any corruption in the police, however minimal it may be, that it only reflects the moral values of society. Complete integrity is taken for granted in many other occupations. Men and women are not forced to join the police force: if they choose to, they must have absolutely honest standards.

EVIDENCE

DOGBERRY: One word, sir: our watch, sir, hath indeed comprehended two aspicious persons, and we would have them this morning examined before your worship.

LEONATO: Take their examination yourself, and bring it me.

(*Much Ado About Nothing*, Act 3, Scene 5)

There is a natural temptation for policemen to feel that they, and not the courts, are the best judges of guilt. In the great majority of cases it is true that they are: their standard is so high in this country that probably nine out of ten people who appear in court are guilty, and the only issue at the trial is whether the guilt can be proved. People are inclined to forget that the police have not only to discover the criminal, but also to produce quickly enough

[1] The 1929 Royal Commission reported: 'The fact that the sentence may be varied as a consequence of statements made by the police in effect puts into their hands a power which it is undesirable they should possess.'

evidence upon which to convict him: few of the inspired guesses of fiction's detectives would have been provable in court. It is highly frustrating for policemen to see their careful work ruined in court by a naïve jury or an incompetent prosecution; it is even more galling for them to listen passively while the defendant and his witnesses lie freely. There are far too few prosecutions for perjury in our courts, despite the difficulties involved. If some of the witnesses who concoct false alibis were prosecuted the police might feel less handicapped. Many police officers naturally resent the licence which is given the defendant in court to perjure and to jeopardize their careers by making malicious allegations.

A completely fabricated case from a policeman is almost unknown, but there is a much stronger temptation for him to embellish his evidence.[1] A policeman rationalized the moral, if not the legal, innocence of bolstering prosecution evidence in this way: 'The public are demanding crime be suppressed. If we know X is guilty, and he's too crafty to give us the evidence we need, is it so important that our evidence conforms to strict reality?' 'All right, guv, it's a fair cop,' once monotonously stated to be a part of defen-

---

[1] The 1960 Royal Commission reported: 'There was a body of evidence, too substantial to disregard, which in effect accused the police of stooping to the use of undesirable means of obtaining statements and of occasionally giving perjured evidence in a court of law. Thus the Law Society suggested that occasionally police officers colour, exaggerate, or even fabricate the evidence against an accused person. These criticisms applied, in their view, only to isolated cases.' The 1929 Commission said: 'Responsible witnesses, with experience on the Bench, have stated that there is occasionally a tendency on the part of the police, when they genuinely believe a prisoner to be guilty, to strain the evidence against him to secure a conviction. This danger is greatest in charges of a vague character, such as "loitering with intent to commit a felony" or indecent behaviour.'

dants' statements, is dying out, though the equally improbable 'Fair enough' is having a brief vogue in what criminals call 'Yardese'. In 1960 a Committee of the Surrey and South London Sessions Bar asked that the whole of the then Flying Squad should be changed because of their 'verbals'. It is even easier to be selective when recounting the defendant's statement, and to disregard what does not fit in with certainty of his guilt, than it is 'to put on the verbals'. One retired police inspector, who has now become a solicitor, said in this connexion that 'It took three or four years out of the force for me to realize what closed minds we had'. One opportunity for *suppressio veri* occurs when sending evidence for forensic analysis: Mr Justice Salmon said in a case in December 1963 that he hoped that the practice of keeping silent about a negative finding was not common and would never happen again. Not all police officers are as particular as others when they attribute 'crimes to be taken into consideration' to the correct defendant: some have been known to agree to put in a good word in return for help in clearing up their books.

The police sometimes feel bitter towards lawyers who attack them in court: one solicitor who threw doubt recently on a policeman's statement about the 'rear door of a Mini-car' was told that 'he was not performing a public service'. 24 per cent of officers who were questioned said that they thought lawyers attacked them unfairly in court, and another 28 per cent thought that they did so sometimes. A number of barristers and solicitors allege that the police have vetoed their doing any more prosecution work, as a result of their cross-examination of police witnesses. The Bench is less rarely complained about: 78 per cent of police officers said they thought that Judges and magistrates were fair to them. Indeed some policemen said that they thought that magistrates were sometimes over-helpful, by, for example, invariably granting adjournments in order to allow the police to reprepare their evidence. An ex-chief inspector said: 'There is no surer way to ruin the police than by supporting them against the weight of the evidence'; one Q.C. who sits as a Recorder commented, 'Nothing can do more good than for the Judge to come down hard on police lying in the witness-box'. But not everybody subscribes to this view: some non-policemen criticize police malpractices (in the same way as they criticize the Suez operation) not for being immoral but for inefficiency in failing. Their reasoning is that they do not wish to undermine confidence in the police; unlike most intelligent policemen, they fail to realize that it is the attempts to gloss over which have this effect. A member of a jury has written:

> After the first day of my fortnight's jury service, I found that most of my fellow jurors believed in the general integrity of the police. Yet after three days I did not find a single juryman in my own court whose faith in the police had not been shaken. We had seen them blush under oath, and the law turned into an ass; in the witness-box they were some-times as much tied into knots by the prosecuting as the defending counsel. In a straight issue between their word and the accused's we invariably gave the benefit of the doubt to the latter. Daily we grew more suspicious of their evidence, and often the verdicts that we returned were based on considerations which, strictly speaking, were nothing to do with what we heard.[1]

Policemen should not feel that it is a personal slight on them for costs to be awarded to a defendant. The expres-sion 'costs against the police' should be dropped: the

[1] Neville Braybrooke, *New Statesman*, 8 June 1962.

police's supreme duty is to obtain justice, not a conviction. Verbal evidence even at best is a tenuous account of a past event, by the time it has been subconsciously edited by the mind of a witness and the ears of jurymen. One police officer said, 'Everything reported, even by truthful witnesses, is wrong'. It is doubtful how much police notebooks fulfil any useful probative purpose (especially since Mr Justice Byrne allowed two or more policemen to synthesize their entries), unless the defendant has read and signed the entry at the earliest opportunity: a record made an hour or two later by anybody is rarely accurate. Yet it is disturbingly rare for a policeman, once he has grown accustomed to taking the oath and to giving evidence, ever to admit any human uncertainty in the witness-box. A police officer is in a terrible conflict when called upon to verify a lying colleague; though one Special said he knew an officer who acted as an 'understudy' in the witness-box for a colleague who had gone on holiday.

Part of justice the conviction of the guilty, and it is essential for juries to be satisfied about the truth of statements and witnesses. Under the present system, a premium in a prosecution is put upon the integrity of the police. Some forces, such as Hertfordshire, have a reputation for being conspicuously fair towards the defence. The majority of policemen are worthy of their responsibility; years of undermanning and overwork in a losing battle have affected some of the few who are not. But people who break as well as those who observe the law have their rights, and their problems have been highlighted recently through the prosecution of many reliable citizens who are motorists or political demonstrators. The tenacity, finances, and previous good character of some of these defendants have enabled them to make exposures in a way denied to the usual criminal. In one case, expensive analyses enabled a man to prove that some spit on a jacket, which was the main prosecution evidence, did not originate from himself. In another recent disturbing series of cases, only by incurring considerable scientific expenses (which were not refunded by the court) were several young men able to secure their acquittals on charges brought by some police officers at West End Central Police Station in London, alleging that they had had half-bricks in their pockets at a demonstration against the Greek queen in July 1963. Compensation and reinvestigation of these cases by the police came too grudgingly and too late: over three months of parliamentary and legal agitation were necessary before the possibility of injustice was recognized.

VIOLENCE

LEAR: Thou rascal beadle, hold thy bloody hand!
Why dost thou lash that whore? Strip thine own back:
Thou hotly lust'st to use her in that kind
For which thou whipp'st her. The usurer hangs the cozener.
Through tatter'd clothes small vices do appear;
Robes and furr'd gowns hide all. Plate sin with gold,
And the strong lance of justice hurtless breaks;
Arm it in rags, a pigmy's straw doth pierce it.
None doth offend, none, I say none. . . .
              (*King Lear*, Act 4, Scene 6)

Although it is difficult to estimate the incidence, police officers and criminals say that violence by the police is even rarer than corruption or perjury. Policemen and criminals both accept that they run occupational risks, and seldom complain in court of violence. 112 officers from West End Central Police Station alone were assaulted in 1962. No member of the public can expect an unarmed policeman to tackle an armed criminal without using force, and a police officer who fails to make an arrest or allows an escape is liable to find himself on a serious disciplinary charge. The police's opponents are bound by no Queensberry rules. Although people are often sceptical when they hear 'he became violent and had to be restrained', a very high proportion of police violence is the result of some verbal or physical provocation. Occasionally criminals start a fight in order to have bruises which they can show the jury; more often they like to exaggerate to give themselves a heroic aura instead of the ignominious one of being caught. A small minority of people joined in recent political demonstrations in order to bait the police; the brunt of the C.N.D. offensive fell on the policemen who lost their leave.

On the other hand, reports of the conduct of some plain-clothed *agents provocateurs* and police smashing cameras on occasions are sinister; and the crowd in Downing Street at the time of Suez was perfectly good-tempered until it began to be squeezed by mounted police. Policemen like their horses so strongly that they react violently when they fear attacks upon them. Mounted police are now an anachronism, and do more harm than good in the delicate relationship with crowds.

One retired Metropolitan inspector (who is perhaps not typical, because before joining the police he had been a pugilist, barman, and boxing-instructor) wrote:

> One way and another I suppose I have had some forty battles with customers. If they started it they were naturally charged with assault. If I felt that I had been the aggressive one, then the most they had to fear was a charge of obstructing an officer in the execution of his duty, never assault. That was an unwritten law that I hope still runs.

Police violence, when it does occur, must be viewed in the context of the climate of our society, and in particular among the masculine *mores* of the world which the police share with prison officers and criminals. Some policemen are as emotionally involved against crime as religious crusaders.[1] Indignation and strain on occasions cause their repressed tension to break out in aggression. Some of them frankly enjoy fighting, in the way a schoolboy or a soldier does. Many policemen are opposed to violence, but have violent feelings within themselves which are brought to the surface by frustration. One very senior retired C.I.D. chief seriously offered as his solution to the crime problem that '45,000 decent Englishmen should march on the prisons and string up the inmates'. Psychiatrists say that we wish to destroy in our enemies what we are unable to stomach in ourselves.

Aggression has never lacked rationalization. A policeman, in particular, needs to excuse his anti-social conduct if his life is not to be meaningless. One of the main police participants in the recent Sheffield affair said that he felt that beating such as that was certainly justified – 'the hardened type of criminal will not respond to the normal methods of detection and therefore probably a good hiding or a beating is the only solution'; he then began an irrelevant diatribe against policemen's special anathema, sex criminals:

> I think in sexual crimes where little girls are being violated, I think they are justified then. When a detective or

[1] An ex-detective superintendent wrote: 'I love the thrill of the chase. There's a warm satisfaction which rises inside of me when I sit in a court room and hear the Judge pronounce sentence.' In some other memoirs, an ex-inspector has written: 'I enjoyed every arrest I made, from simple drunks to life-sentence felons . . . but I seldom loved the prisoners.'

184

any person goes home and sees his little daughter asleep on the pillow then I – it's hard to explain how one feels – the revulsion at these crimes. I think that a beating is the only answer to turn a man from this type of crime.

Although generally policemen say that it is no concern of theirs what sentence a criminal receives, others consider it should be part of their function to add a 'rough time' to the court's sentence when, for example, they know extra information about an offender from their informers. Some prisoners give as their reason for not complaining that 'the police can make a lot of difference to your life when you're out'. Men sometimes allege that they have been hit in the small of their back or on the back of their neck so as to leave no marks; signs of violence on prisoners are certainly very rare. The most common occasions are when a policeman has been injured, in spite of the fact that this is already a special legal offence.

Violence in any circumstances is unhesitatingly condemned by the majority of policemen: 'There is no excuse for a policeman ever assaulting a prisoner, however tempted,' said the Secretary of the Police Federation. Fortunately in this country force and threats generally result in acquittal; the law insists that confessions must be entirely free and voluntary. We have never here had the hose-piping and sweat-box of the Third Degree. Not only are the means never justified by the ends, but they also often lead to false confessions. In the words of one senior C.I.D. officer: 'Hitting's not the slightest use: it only makes men tell you what they think you want to hear; what you need is subterfuge to get at the truth'.

Physical violence is easy to define and exclude; but it is more difficult to draw the borderline where mental pressure becomes oppressive. Some police officers regard alcohol as a justifiable ally to help loosen tongues. One constable even recounted with pride how he and some colleagues once extorted a confession from two West Indians by staging a mock trial at the police station, sentencing them to death, and leading them to an adjoining room where they were told they would be hanged immediately.

It goes without saying that this is exceptional, and so, according to every source, is the incident at Sheffield on 14 March 1963. It is worth while to examine in some detail the genesis and lessons of this episode, which was as incredible to many policemen as to most of the public. The Sheffield force had not increased its establishment since 1947. Its C.I.D. was in fact actually reduced in size between 1953 and 1958, while crime increased by 25 per cent. As a result, its fifty detectives in 1962 worked more than 16,000 hours of unpaid overtime, for which they could not be compensated by time off in lieu. The Report of the subsequent Inquiry conducted by a Q.C. and an Inspector of Constabulary says that:

> The minds of the appellants were already conditioned by the dangerous notion they had formed that a Crime Squad was a *corps d'élite* which could use tough methods to deal with tough criminals and take risks to achieve speedy results. . . . Mr Streets . . . told us that he held views that criminals are treated far too softly by the Courts, that because criminals break rules, police may and must do so to be a jump ahead.

The Inquiry found that the mitigation for the two detective constables who carried out 'deliberate, unprovoked, brutal, and sustained assaults, with weapons in the nature of a truncheon and a short flexible piece of gut-like material, upon prisoners who were defenceless and did not

retaliate, for the purpose of inducing confessions of crime'
was:

(*a*) they had been working long hours and were over-
tired and hungry;

(*b*) they were, and felt, under pressure to obtain results;

(*c*) their use of violence had been encouraged by hints
beforehand, and it had been instituted and witnessed with
approval by senior officers;

(*d*) that these senior officers and another detective constable who joined in the violence were wholly inadequately
dealt with by the chief constable;

(*e*) that they had been told to give a false account in
court by a senior officer, who concocted it.

The 'gut-like material' to which the Inquiry referred
was a rhinoceros whip that one of the detective constables
had appropriated from the offensive weapons which had
been handed in to the police, and which he said he carried
'in case of conflicts between coloured informants'. With it,
together with an old-type truncheon, and several fists, four
men were beaten in relays, one of them with up to seventy
blows in five separate and successive beatings. The detective inspector who watched and 'displayed callous amuse-
ment' told the Inquiry 'these things go on fairly frequently,
don't they'. The Inquiry concluded that he had thought
an assaulted man 'would be unlikely to complain or to be
believed if he did'.

When the victims did complain in court, the Inquiry
recorded that nobody in the Sheffield force took any
action for at least five days, with the result that the officers
involved were able to burn the two weapons. The victims'
solicitor was told misleading statements; the Crime Squad
concocted lying stories and even fabricated evidence; the

detective chief inspector who was deputed to investigate 'commiserated with them'. The chief constable who, the Inquiry found, was 'over-obsessed with the bogey of publicity' and 'shut his eyes to the evidence', when he purported to reprimand the officers, shook them by their hands.

From the Report[1] (which should be required reading for all police officers, magistrates, and members of Police Authorities, as well as the members of the Willink Commission) it is clear that the tragedy had its roots in overwork and the lack of standards set by the senior C.I.D. officers at Sheffield. It is unlikely that such open assaults would have taken place unless the junior officers felt confident that they were safe from disciplinary proceedings. But the greatest lesson of the Sheffield Inquiry (and it is one of the virtues of such inquiries that constructive lessons for the future can be learnt from them) is that it should have been inconceivable that, within one month of its description of the police inquiries in that case, the Home Secretary would introduce a Police Bill proposing to leave similar inquiries in the hands of the police.

INQUIRIES

After the publication of the Sheffield Report, it must have been patently obvious to everybody in Britain, other apparently than Mr Brooke, that the public could in future only be satisfied by inquiries where someone independent was present. One Chairman of Quarter Sessions said that after it he had found that juries were much less willing to accept police evidence: not because of the violence itself, but because of the ease with which it was shown that covering-up and perjury could take place.

[1] H.M.S.O., price 2s. 3d.

Most allegations are investigated by the police vigorously ('too thoroughly', commented some policemen, though others denied that this is possible). The Metropolitan Commissioner said that he thought that more policemen are found guilty under the present system than would be by an impartial outside tribunal, even if it had the power to subpoena and hear evidence on oath. These powers would be essential: the Tribunal who investigated the Thurso case went out of its way to point out that it had been able to determine the truth (that a constable, despite his denials, had struck the boy John Waters) only because it had had power to call the police as witnesses; and that in a court where they could decline to be cross-examined their word would probably have been preferred to the boy's.

The figures show that, at present, guilt is virtually certain when a disciplinary inquiry is held: in 1962, 243 officers were punished in the Metropolitan Force, compared with only 8 who were found not guilty. Outside London 969 were found guilty out of 1,061 – and only 8 were aggrieved enough by the result to exercise their right of appeal.

The Willink Commission's and Mr Brooke's only excuse for rejecting independent inquiries has been the damage it might cause to police morale; but this last plank has been removed, because several chief constables and a majority of policemen would in fact welcome them to convince the public that justice is being seen to be done. The chief constable, who holds the inquiry under the present system, is in the invidious position of being at the same time judge and jury and of having initiated the prosecution, as well as being a quasi-defendant because he is responsible for the state of the force. Some police officers would prefer an inquiry to have an independent chairman because a chief constable often has personal views on each of his men. There is often only a hair's breadth separating commendation for meritorious work and punishment for excess of zeal; if a lawyer was present at disciplinary inquiries, he could see fair play for both sides.

Minor matters could continue to be dealt with inside the force as at present. But a dissatisfied member of the public should have the same right of appeal as a policeman enjoys at present. The actual machinery which would hear the appeal is a matter of detail that should not be allowed to delay the adoption of the principle. At the moment, the protests go to M.P.s, the N.C.C.L., and *Justice* (an all-party collective conscience of the legal profession),[1] none of whom has any facilities for investigation. The most satisfactory solution would be a national Ombudsman, who could also hear allegations, for example, against prison officers and indeed in any matter where the complainant is at a disadvantage against somebody who is all-powerful. (At present the Home Office often refused to allow a prisoner to institute proceedings, for example, for assaults; its excuse that 'he can do so when he is released' is absurd in cases where witnesses are unobtainable years later.) The chief constables suggested to the Willink Commission a combination of a County Court Judge and an outside chief constable. Others have proposed a Commissioner of Rights, or regional tribunals with an experienced legal chairman and a senior police officer as assessor. The tribunal need not necessarily sit in open court if that is contrary to public interest; and it should have power to award costs, in order to discourage malicious attacks. As a protection for the police officers involved, their names

[1] Crane Court, Fleet St., EC4.

should not be published unless and until they are found guilty.

The complainant should be allowed to be present and should be able to cross-examine witnesses. This was recommended by a Royal Commission on the Metropolitan Police as long ago as 1906, which said:

> The question of how such complaints ought to be dealt with is, in our opinion, one of great importance, because the maintenance of good relations between the police and the rest of the community largely depends upon the existence among law-abiding persons of the confident belief that any grievances they may have in connection with the behaviour and exercise of authority by members of the police will be respectfully received, promptly and effectively inquired into, and, so far as possible, remedied. . . . We do not think that the existing method of inquiry into complaints made against the police by private persons is satisfactory. . . .
>
> We think: The complainant should be invited to attend at New Scotland Yard or a convenient police staion and to bring with him any witnesses, and the accused member of the force should be ordered to attend with his witnesses . . . the complainant and the accused respectively should have the right to cross-examine witnesses directly.

Those who argue that these inquiries would place men in jeopardy twice over forget that members of other professions, such as journalists, doctors, lawyers, and dentists, already face complaints before similar tribunals, sometimes with a layman as chairman. In Philadelphia, a board composed of citizens has been established to hear allegations of racialism or violence against the police, and it has been found that it both satisfies complainants and markedly improves the police's standing in the community. In all probability, machinery for independent inquiries would hardly ever be used: its mere existence would be sufficient to discourage any conduct or covering-up such as took place at Sheffield. The Ombudsman, who has functioned successfully as a tonic for the bureaucracy and police in Denmark for eight years, has not once needed to exercise his power to order a prosecution.

The reason why all major inquiries should be independent are perfectly clear, and are the same as those urged by *Justice* in support of an Ombudsman: (*a*) No department or authority should be the judge in its own cause; (*b*) a complainant has a natural sense of frustration if he has his complaint rejected without being given the opportunity of putting his facts before an impartial tribunal and without being informed of the evidence by which his complaint was refuted; (*c*) if complaints are impartially investigated, the department and its officers are able to clear themselves of wild and unfounded charges made against them, and a greater degree of confidence and mutual respect is established between public servants and the public.

Many people have no wish to risk an expensive court action or to get damages against a police officer, but only desire to pursue their complaints from a sense of injustice, whether justified or not. Lord Devlin has said, 'It is the general habit of the police never to admit to the slightest departure from correctness'. They are not the only people to share this characteristic. It would be better if both civil servants and policemen felt that they were allowed to admit that they are human, and that to do so would not necessarily prejudice their job. Some police discipline at the moment is too strict and military; an independent inquiry should make every allowance for mistakes committed in the public interest. In addition, chief constables should make available maliciously false letters of allegation, so that police officers could pursue their right to sue for libel in the same way as anybody else.

In some individual cases in the past, senior officers have been reluctant and slow to investigate because of fear of publicity and an illusion that to do so would sap public confidence in the police generally. Since the Second World War, Home Secretaries have set up an independent inquiry into a police matter on six occasions (two of which were in the last half of 1963). But their establishment at present comes about through haphazard mixtures of chance and pressure. Sheffield only came fully to light, after eight months, because of a combination of a determined solicitor, an active newspaper, corroborative wounds on the victims, and the unexpected decision of the two dismissed detectives to appeal. When Mr Brooke eventually did set up an inquiry several months after *Justice* asked him to do so, he established one in a form which was unjust to several of the people implicated, who were unable to cross-examine or answer allegations made against them. At independent inquiries in the future, every party concerned in a case should be represented and receive natural justice.

The overdue introduction of independent inquiries would do more than anything else to dispel the suspicion between the police and the public, which we shall examine in the next chapter. Their findings would produce constructive lessons which could benefit police forces all over the country. It would also give greater justice to the police themselves, in their vulnerable job. If an independent investigator had been able to announce quickly the truth about the episodes in Trafalgar Square on 17 September 1961, about Harold Woolf, about the evidence of Miss Ricardo in the Ward case, or even about Sheffield or the half-bricks, immense damage would have been spared the police force.

CHAPTER 8

The Public and the Police

The police will always need to be resigned to suffering more complaints than any other profession or service: uniquely, in their case efficiency is often as little welcomed as inefficiency because of the 'sheepdog' paradox that was examined in Chapter One. In addition to their being exposed in the same way as doctors or lawyers to allegations that they have fallen short of their duty, the police receive nearly twice as many complaints that they have exceeded their duty in some way. Chief constables estimate that the proportion which has any foundation is only 10–25 per cent. A considerable number of the allegations made by motorists and criminals may be conscious or subconscious attempts to justify misconduct on their own part. It is not surprising that some policemen become stoically immune to criticism, for the demands that the public make are often conflicting and incompatible: an officer is told to 'clean up all vice' and at the same time to 'make allowances for human nature'. And the client of a brothel may be the very same man who is most vocal in complaining about the toleration of an abortionist.

A car-driver, who is angry at other motorists who exceed the speed limit when he himself is not doing so, is often equally indignant when the positions are reversed. One in three of the complaints against the police arise out of their duties in connexion with traffic. Motoring is most often

194

blamed by members of the public who feel that relations with the police have deteriorated: in the Social Survey, more non-motorists (84·1 per cent) than motorists (79·9 per cent) said they had 'great respect' for the police. People who consider themselves law-abiding reveal unexpected characteristics when driving. 755,753 people were prosecuted and 735,049 were found guilty of motoring offences in 1962 – about seven for every 100 vehicles on the road. The police themselves regret and are apprehensive about this trend as much as anybody. In June 1959 the Metropolitan Commissioner relaxed minor traffic prosecutions in an effort to remove 'factors tending to inflame a sense of hostility against the police'. Overworked officers today completely agree with the motorists' refrain: 'Why don't you catch criminals instead of persecuting us?' In 1962 and 1963, the Southend-on-Sea police have dealt with 300 traffic offenders by explaining their faults to them and, in some cases, giving them advanced driving lessons instead of by taking them to court.

Other unwelcomed contacts with the police, however, are also on the increase: out of every 100,000 males in England and Wales, 895 were found guilty of indictable crimes in 1962, compared with only 393 per 100,000 in 1938. There has also been a rise in the other categories of offences among people who do not normally regard themselves as enemies of the police. A recent inquiry estimated that shoplifting has increased by 40 per cent in the last five years, and the numbers of people being prosecuted for tax-evasion and for not paying their fare when travelling are all-time records. In 1962, 83,992 people were arrested for drunkenness – more than in any previous year, and an increase of 12·5 per cent on 1961. Recent demonstrations have involved another and new section of the population, some of them holding strong civic principles, and many of whom are at a young and formative age. In addition, immigration has augmented the minority groups who find most difficulty in integrating into the community (more than three out of ten people convicted of assaults on policemen are immigrants).

Even law-abiding people have always had a curiously ambivalent attitude towards policemen and criminals. Universal hostility greeted the earliest police officers: today people often seem reluctant to take sides in what they tend to regard as a private war between police and criminals. In High Wycombe in October 1963, fifty men and women stood and watched while three men fought the police and broke the arm of one constable; only one woman actually gave any help to the police. The British fear of getting involved may often be due to unwillingness to act as a witness, but it can also go deeper. People sometimes think that an offence does not constitute a sufficient threat to society; they may have a sneaking envy or sympathy for the criminal. Smugglers have always been more popular than customs officers. We associate crimes with forbidden pleasures, and also feel a lack of identification with, for example, a bank that has been robbed. People are attracted by the 'sporting' element in crime, particularly if no vilence is used: some of them boast of diddling the tax inspector or the storekeeper at their factory. Many modern business practices can be viewed as 'white-collar crime' – socially accepted delinquent activity.

It is interesting that women instinctively rely on and support the police to a far greater extent than men do. They are estimated to make over 70 per cent of all 999 calls. Whether this is through being innately less criminal, or because they have an instinct to protect their home and seek a father-figure, research would be needed to show. By contrast, it may offend masculine pride to call a policeman for help. One businessman recently boasted to his friends for five weeks that he could cope with some unknown men who were following him; he didn't tell the police until he had been coshed and robbed of £2,000.

Despite these factors, and the gloomy fears of policemen themselves, their relations with the public in general remain very good. 82·7 per cent of people who were asked by the Social Survey in 1960 said they had 'great respect' for the police. In 1950 Mr Geoffrey Gorer asked readers of *The People* the question: 'What do you think of the police?' An analysis of 5,000 answers, picked at random from the 11,000 he received, showed that 73·5 per cent were 'appreciative', compared with only 5 per cent who were described as 'hostile' and who included 1 per cent who were 'almost pathological'. The replies included many similar to that of the labourer who described them as 'over-worked underpaid men with a high sense of duty. One of the chief reasons why this is such a pleasant country to live in'. Another man wrote: 'At the beginning of my life, I hated them on sight, I have been in trouble as a youth; now however with home, wife and children I cherish, I would risk my life to help them in any circumstances.' The Royal Commission's Social Survey questioned nobody under 18; but in Gorer's sample the proportion of younger people who were in favour of the police was higher than the average among all ages: 82 per cent of those aged under 18, and 75 per cent of those aged 18–24.[1]

In the face of this evidence, it is interesting to ask why there is such pessimism and alarm among the police them-

[1] G. Gorer: *Exploring English Character* (Cresset Press, 1955).

selves concerning their relations with the public. Even after the reassurance of the Royal Commission, 58 per cent of policemen who were asked in 1963 how they thought relations between the police and the public were now, compared with before the war, replied that they were worse, compared with 10 per cent who said they were better and 12 per cent who said they were the same. The Social Survey suggested one reason for this:

> There is a further not inconsiderable disadvantage in police work, and this is the burden of social isolation that the police feel their position carries. This isolation is experienced not only by the police themselves but to some extent by their wives and children as well. In these respects police work is probably unique. It follows that the police are continually in a defensive position and any real or imagined criticism from individuals or sections of the general public, the press, or authorities such as the courts or members of parliament is liable to produce in the police mind a distorted impression of what the public in general feel about them. There is no way in which the police can assess changes of opinion in their favour, as praise is less likely to be expressed than criticism.

This feeling of isolation is greatest in urban areas. The Survey reported:

> There were marked differences between the opinions of police serving in the large towns and those in other urban and rural districts, with a higher proportion of the police in the large towns thinking that there had been changes for the worse in the attitudes not only of the public but also of the police. There were also differences in the opinions of longer and shorter-service police, with the longer-service police in general being more dissatisfied and more critical in their assessment of the situation.

Such feelings can be carried to extraordinary degrees.

One inspector, who had served for twenty years in the Metropolitan force, wrote when he retired: 'Few people other than dear old ladies and foreigners really liked the London policeman. The vast majority longed to score off him. Many feared and hated him as much as he feared and hated them.' Serving policemen say that 'the public dislike us until they need our help', and that 'the public stand by and leave it all to a policeman, and are then delighted when he goes wrong so that they can complain'. Some officers speak bitterly of the public's lack of loyalty, and say that journalists and lawyers often make them feel that it is the police who are on trial instead of the criminal. Others wondered if they themselves are not affected by only thinking of the public in terms of drunks, perverts, nuisances, or complainants. One young officer in London said that when the public always appeared to be dependent on him for elementary information about the way or the time, it was easy for him to get to feel that the public are fools and the police are superior.

The most frequent complaint made by a policeman against members of the public is that they forget they have a duty to help the police, though the same people are never slow to remember their rights. In the Social Survey, 87 per cent of the police considered that the public did not do enough to help them (and 75 per cent of the public who were questioned agreed). Greater wealth has caused more people to insure their property and not to worry unduly about its loss. Many stores today do nothing to discourage shoplifting: a few even say that they are pleased when it occurs because it proves the attractiveness of their open-shelf display. People, unless their own or their friends' property is threatened, are reluctant to interfere and report suspicious circumstances: the civic responsibility of British people in peacetime so often extends only to people they know, and stops short of the full community. This is a problem which any government should tackle urgently. Not only might those who show courage by going to the help of the police figure more in the Honours List and receive more generous compensation if they are injured,[1] but the subject of civics should be part of every school curriculum. The tiny series of advertisements by the police urging people to lock their windows and cars are a half-hearted failure. Far too little is spent by the police on communicating with the public: full-scale use should be made of B.B.C. radio and television, together with the press and cinemas, to gain their co-operation and help. The chief constable of Southend has started with great success to hold regular conferences at police headquarters in order to exchange views with local inhabitants on problems of security. It would also pay the police to follow up and personally thank people who did help them: one man who has given them assistance on six occasions during his life complained that he had never heard the outcome of any of the cases.

Relations between the police and the public have not necessarily worsened in recent years, but they have altered. Both bodies have become more distant and less human to each other as they have both become increasingly urbanized and motorized. Even if he is not affected by being a motorist himself, the man in the street is not in contact with a policeman in a patrol car. The trend is seen carried to an even further degree in the United

---

[1] At present there is no formal right to any compensation for damage or injury suffered by somebody helping the police.

States. Studies there have shown that public attitudes towards the police are primarily the result of personal contacts between individual citizens and police officers, and the evidence in this country is that both are suffering from increasing isolation from each other. Police relations here on the whole tend to be better in rural communities and small towns, and at their worst in the cities and London: in the village the policeman is still known by his name as 'Mr —', whereas in the city he is an anonymous figure in uniform. Police officers say that the most difficult districts of all are the new housing estates – 'no community spirit and no informers', one detective-constable complained in a voice of despair.

It is important for both sides that this growing loss of contact should be halted and reversed. An imaginative attempt to do this has been started by two forces, who have split up new town areas into 'neighbourhoods', each of which is assigned a particular police officer whose name is published and whom people are encouraged to know as a human individual. Started by West Sussex at Crawley, the scheme has now been successfully extended to Hemel Hempstead, Stevenage and Welwyn by Hertfordshire. The present size of each police officer's neighbourhood is 5,000 people; if it were closer to 1,500 this would be an excellent method of splitting up all urban areas. In order to bridge the personal gulf, the neighbourhood officer could announce regular times and places where he could be contacted, while other police maintained crime and traffic patrols.

It is inevitable that 'sheep never like their sheepdog', as one chief constable has said (he continued: 'What is public opinion? What is it worth?'). Most policemen disagree, but too often only in a negative and defensive way. It is a disciplinary offence for a police officer to be uncivil to a member of the public; but the Police Federation says that 'the police service has not yet recognized that there is a public image of the police'. 'It's the public who need to learn about good relations, not us,' one senior officer stated. 'Too many chief constables are still living in the Victorian era,' a policeman remarked, 'and just believe in shutting up and saying nothing.' Mr William Shepherd said in the House of Commons during the debate on the Royal Commission's Report: 'I feel very strongly that the police have too closed a mind, and lead too monastic an existence, to get the right sort of relationship with the public. Policemen of great quality sometimes behave – because of the particular nature of their association with each other – in a way which I find almost impossible to understand.' In some forces 'public relations' still have the appearance of being regarded as dirty words; if they are to have any effect they must be tackled positively and not defensively. Various government departments in the last few years have gradually come to realize that they must take the initiative in order to gain public goodwill; the police are almost alone now in lacking a central department able to do this and to reply to criticism. Much more could also be done by the police in announcing to the public reasons and explanations for their policies whenever possible.

The police in other forces are trying different solutions to the same problem. In Paris, a magazine called *Liaison* has been started with the purpose of explaining to the public what are the problems of the police. The criminologist who was appointed head of the Munich force in 1963 has called in a psychiatrist to teach his men better relations with the public; the Japanese police take an annual survey of public opinions concerning them. In November 1963 the chief constable of Brighton suggested that his force should appoint a public relations police officer whose job would be to make everybody feel that the police were giving them a fair deal. Contact on a personal level will always, however, remain the most important. Policemen should take every opportunity of exchanging views with the public in clubs, universities, schools, and on the radio and television. The Special constables, who have a foot in each camp, can play an important part in explaining to both sides the problems and points of friction: it may be significant that, for every hundred regulars, there are only 15 Specials in London and 40 in other cities and boroughs, compared with 120 in county forces.

Public interest in police matters is enormous: the audience for *Z Cars* is nearly 16 million; over a thousand people went to visit Limehouse police station when it held an 'open day' in 1963. The public have a right to know more about the police which they pay for. At present it is largely left to novelists and script-writers to supply impressions and knowledge about the police to the public; some forces have a detrimental cult of unnecessary secretiveness.

In some cases this secrecy is due to fear in the police that crime might be encouraged by knowledge about themselves. The whole force is also proud of its tradition that they 'hear all, see all, and say nothing'. It is greatly to their credit that their immense knowledge concerning the private details of so many lives is never made public. But the tradition of sealed lips has other, less fortunate, repercussions: it means that people rarely hear anything other than criticism concerning policemen. Their many instances of kindness and humanity are not reported: people never know when a policeman dips into his own pocket to help the family of a man in prison, or finds a job for an old lag after his release. These items have little news-value for newspapers; in addition they are sometimes illegal: one officer who allowed a prisoner on a very grave charge to visit his relative in hospital could have been in serious trouble.

The absence of independent inquiries has led to the ventilation of complaints about the police in Parliament and newspapers. The obduracy and incredulity shown by the police towards some complainants has caused them to feel that the police will only take seriously a writ or a M.P.'s question. Policemen intensely dislike politicians who try to make capital out of incidents concerning them, and many officers have become very sensitive and even hostile towards the press as a result of reading only denigration of themselves. 72 per cent of officers who were asked in 1963 said that they thought that the press were unfair towards the police, together with another 8 per cent who said they were 'sometimes', compared with 14 per cent who said that in the main they were not. Complaints by policemen ranged from exaggerations and twisting of stories to saying that untrue allegations are frequently printed and rarely corrected when they are proved to be false. The Press Council might consider some rule whereby, after a charge against anybody (police or otherwise) has been made and reported, a newspaper should be obliged to report its outcome with equal prominence. Reporters are inclined to forget that individual policemen are unable to reply to allegations: even when a case is not *sub judice*, it is an offence in the police

Disciplinary Code for a police officer to communicate to the public or the press without proper authority. Policemen also complain that their superiors 'do not back them up' sufficiently by challenging allegations or by putting them into their correct perspective before they are blown up into huge proportions. They also blame reporters for not ringing up the authorized police spokesman to hear his version before they rush into print and cause damage that a later denial is never able to repair.

Part of this ill-feeling between the police and the press is caused by lack of understanding about each other's function and difficulties. The main aim of a newspaper (although often the last reason it gives) is to sell copies. News – and the police are always news—must be printed quickly or not at all. When the police are asked for their version of some story, it is frequently not forthcoming for several days, either because the matter is *sub judice* (as, for example, in the case of Podola) or because it takes time for them to make a thorough investigation. By the time a refutation or explanation is available newspapers feel it has little interest for readers.

With certain crime reporters whom they know and trust, the police have working relationships; sometimes they feed them exclusive news in exchange for information (reporters can and do give witnesses money to speak, when the police cannot). The men police complaints are chiefly directed against are the sub-editors, whom they feel are frequently only interested in building up a sensation, and irresponsibly tend to ignore the wider implications of how they present news about the police or a criminal. Some senior police officers believe that crime is encouraged by newspapers glamourizing it and describing successful methods; others feel that a few papers are actually malicious towards the police by reporting them only in such a way as to give the impression 'that they are never able to put a boot right'. Both sides are resentful because of each other's lack of co-operation in the past, though on occasions, when the police have taken them into their confidence the press have helped by withholding a story or by keeping the search for somebody in the public attention. Police forces in general have a good relationship with their local newspaper, because each depends on and has learnt to live with the other. The degree of liaison depends on the individual chief constable: some have appointed a public relations and a press officer; others remain deeply suspicious of either. The editor of one national newspaper said that he preferred to deal with a policeman rather than a professional public relations man; it is essential in order to do the job successfully that the holder should know the workings of both the police and the press, and also should have the confidence of his chief constable.

Relations with the press should be part of police training. A bureau is also needed which could speak on behalf of the police nationally: at present they suffer because forces and ranks are fragmented and each is unable to speak for all. The Home Office has always been reluctant to arouse suspicions of central interference; the Police Federation do not possess the facts; and the chief constables meet only occasionally.

At present not only the best, but virtually the only attempt to increase public understanding about the police is being done by two B.B.C. television programmes. Views about the police – like those about other minority groups – tend to become stereotyped. People forget that inside police uniforms are human characters, perhaps young and inexperienced or tired and worried. One of the virtues of *Z Cars* (although the episodes are too well written to convey the monotony of much police life) is that without patronizing them it shows policemen as individuals with problems in relationships among themselves as well as towards the outside world. Many serving police officers think that the programme gives 'as accurate a picture of police-life (in the north) as you are likely to get', and often they watch it compulsively. *Dixon of Dock Green* on the other hand they describe as 'an overgrown Boy Scout looking for his good deed'. 'It's a good image, but it doesn't fool anyone nowadays,' said one serving P.C.; an inspector added, 'It's about as far away from actual police life as you can imagine.' *Dixon* is as unreal as *Perry Mason*, by whom the police are invariably outwitted; but (significantly) some senior police officers have attacked instead the realism of *Z Cars*. 'I hate it,' said one deputy chief constable, 'it shows no respect for the police.' '*Z Cars* is a typical bad example whereas *Dixon* is a good example,' said the chief constable of another force.

In fact, *Z Cars*, by showing the human problems and tensions of the police, can do them nothing but good: realism is just what public thinking about both the police and crime so badly needs.

The Future of the Police

A society will have the police that it deserves. The time has come for realistic and scientific thinking about our police and their problems. Over a period of many years there has been a serious lack of research into every aspect of them: Royal Commissions have been asked to report in a vacuum. Any sizeable commercial firm would make a thorough study of the reasons for its recruitment and wastage. More money is spent in Britain today in preparation for the launching of a new soap-powder than on research into all the problems of our police put together. The Government should no longer hesitate to spend heavily on gaining people's goodwill for public services: it should recognize that to do so would save immeasurable friction and money in future years. Private commercial companies are far more alive to this necessity than public services which are infinitely more essential. It is our old story of private waste and public squalor. A Member of Parliament said: 'I think it is we who have been very largely responsible for the defects in the police.' Only public servants who are unable to strike would have had their pay neglected for as long as that of the police before 1960.

The results of years of parsimony cannot be reversed overnight: their accumulated effect on police manpower means that entry tests at present are still being used more to reject the worst than to select the best of new recruits. Physical health is necessary for a policeman, but modern conditions require that the emphasis in the future must be on brains. I.Q. and temperament tests should be part of a more scientific policy for the selection of recruits. The police themselves are apprehensive about the future that will result from the particularly lean decade of recruiting in the 1950s, when police pay lagged behind industrial earnings throughout the period between demobilization and the Royal Commission. The new courses at Bramshill are commendable efforts to plug the future gaps; but many policemen say that the new approach to training was introduced too late, and reaches men at too late an age to change fixed attitudes.

Wastage is, and is likely to remain an even greater problem than recruitment. Overwork can be reduced if we are prepared to spend more money; but it is also necessary for a policeman to feel that his job is constructive, interesting, and important if he is going to be resilient to its inevitable frustrations. The attractive myth of a policeman being just a member of the public in uniform cannot be continued any longer; in fact he performs a number of professional roles, each of which requires extensive specialized training.

The change that psychology and sociology have brought about in our attitude to criminal behaviour has made the work of policemen more complicated. They too should therefore develop. For their work of prevention they will increasingly need to become agents of social welfare; to succeed in detection they will have to be scientists. One theme recurs throughout the different chapters of this book: it is not the changes in modern society which affect the morale of the police (as the Royal Commission

o

thought), but failures of the police themselves to adapt to those changes. The basic police attitude is one of reluctance to reform – perhaps their life's work of trying to restore the *status quo* induces a conservative outlook. The early training of a policeman should enable him to adjust to new conditions: a knowledge of psychology, for example, would help him in both his fields of preventive and detective work. Our national cult of the amateur has in the past not always allowed policemen sufficient training to give them the many skills which the importance of their job requires. The training itself should progress organically and not be limited by the ideas of the date when a man was recruited: the more senior an officer becomes the more important it is for him to be able to learn about and make use of new developments. In order that he can keep in touch with legal, social, and scientific changes, every policeman should be given a refresher course of one or two weeks a year.

The police will in the future inevitably face many difficulties through being human agents of stability during times of rapid change. Their work has not become easier because people today are less credulous of the simple myth of good men versus bad: one officer complained, 'The younger generation who have grown up since the war is no longer certain it is possible to say what is right or wrong.' At the same time as our society has become more permissive in moral matters, it has also become readier to intervene in other directions – though more uncertain what it should do to the individual when it does intervene. The principle of state interference, in particular in the form of 'public welfare officers' that were mentioned in Chapter One, has been accepted in many fields, but we remain undecided about the means and ends of such intervention. The growth of both trends has complicated the image and work of the police.

The powers of discretion will always cause them to be involved in the administration of justice, but the study and treatment of crime have now become specialized sciences. A police officer in New York described the change in his function, which is similar to what has taken place here: 'In the old days the cop on the beat kept the peace by handing out curbstone justice. The only time he took anything to court was when he couldn't handle it with his night-stick.' At the same time as fulfilling their primary role, that of seeing that crime does not pay, the police could make an enormous contribution to the study of its cure. Before any successful treatment of criminals can be achieved, it is first necessary to diagnose the causes of criminal behaviour; our punishments have lacked success in the past because of our ignorance about what we are trying to cure or prevent. If he were trained so as to be able to analyse his experience, a policeman could provide valuable field reports. The present trend in penal policy towards probation and parole makes such studies of criminals in their settings in the community of greater value than research about them in the artificial environment of institutions.

In the past policemen have tended to be suspicious of progress in penal reform. Contribution by the police to socio-psychiatric research into crime is the modern form of the preventive role which they have always had. Its development should in turn bring benefits to them by helping to decrease the crime problem by which they are faced. If more money was spent by the government on constructive penal treatment, the work of the police would also be lightened; but such policies have low priority among the promises made at election time.

How far the police should develop as active social workers, as distinct from making a passive contribution to the study of criminology, is a more open question. Some police officers and probation officers at present misunderstand each other's role; other policemen are developing formally or instinctively into case-workers hardly distinguishable from probation officers. It is difficult to deny the illogicality of training a man as a police officer and then employing him full-time in a Juvenile Liaison project. But in the same way as prison officers have recently realized, and expressed for their own circumstances, it would enormously improve the morale and standing of the police (as well as the quality of their recruiting) if they were trained to deal with people as skilfully as they are taught to protect property. Police thinking would profit if it came out of its shell and concerned itself with wider questions of their role and human relations. It might be better if the Liberal Studies at Bramshill included more teaching on modern social questions of relevance to today in place of, for instance, the study of ancient Greece and Rome. Since police-life is unable to attract graduates, serving policemen should become graduates instead: officers should be seconded to universities for courses and degrees in the way that army and probation officers are. Abroad, the University of Pennsylvania, for instance, has provided several hundred scholarships for police officers to study administration and human relations.

If the police are to be better trained and able to develop a more constructive role, it will be necessary for them to have more men. Ideally most people would like a police service which is both humane and efficient. But, as its tasks have increased in number and difficulty, it has not been supplied with the equivalent advances in training or equipment to accomplish them. The new Police Bill does nothing to cure the overwork which is responsible for most of the complaints both by and against policemen (it may be significant that there are twice as many complaints against the police per officer in the Metropolitan force as elsewhere). When people do not adequately help or equip the police, the result is that some officers develop their own methods against criminals.

Sentimentality (from which the police themselves are not free, as their 'Black Museum' at Scotland Yard, with its bloodstained floorboards and rope-nooses, shows) has for too long caused maudlin writers to describe criminal behaviour in terms such as 'the art' of murder. Now that crime is increasing at a faster rate than our population, it is time to recognize the human harm it causes and to approach the whole subject scientifically. Having decided which measures are necessary for its prevention and at the same time are compatible with liberty and the protection of the innocent, the gaps should be closed between theory and practice: at present the public square their consciences by playing a criminal with 'sporting' rules, and then making policemen the scapegoats if he is not caught or the rules are broken. One of the principal reasons for the excessive solidarity among policemen which is acting to the public detriment today is their consciousness that they need to employ quasi-legal, and sometimes illegal, means in order to do their work.

Once the police are given adequate powers we must then see that they keep to them. In law-enforcement ends never justify even slightly dubious means: violence or threats undermine a society more surely than the crime they are intended to prevent. A society which resorts to them finishes by being used by them.

It is a tragedy when the admirable bulk of the police service becomes linked with the image of a few bullies: it is vital for the police themselves that such men should be identified and expelled at the earliest possible moment. Their senior officers should remember that even though the prosecution and dismissal of these men is painful, the police must always be judged by the highest standards, because a single policeman has the power to do great harm to other people as well as to the reputation of the force. The maintenance of police morale, however, depends not on whitewash, but on a satisfying conception of the policeman's place in society. Judges, for example, have high standards not because they are intrinsically different men from the people they have to judge but because of their view of their job. The same self-respect is the key to excellence in the police force.

Independent inquiries are inescapable: the police of a country whose law depends on the jury cannot afford to lack the confidence of the public. Every means should be employed to develop this rapport. In the same way as C.I.D. officers at present have too little time to cultivate their vital contacts, so the uniformed officer is tending to grow increasingly distant from the public. Something more than local Police Authorities is needed for the police and the public to understand each other's problems. Now that 80 per cent of Britain's population are living in towns, it has become important that urban police areas should be split up into personal communities; the police as well as town-planners can encourage a sense of belonging in a neighbourhood. It is in the interests of everybody to stop the development of a separate police culture, and to minimize the suspicion and antagonism which becomes mutual between both the police and the public. For their part, the police should attempt to increase their contacts and exchanges with the public on friendly and helpful occasions: work like the crime prevention lectures and driving instruction they are giving in some areas should be extended throughout the country. Seminars should be started where police officers could discuss their ideas and problems. But the gap must be closed from both sides. Policemen have a saying that people 'only remember God and the police when they are in trouble'. The main need is for the public to develop a greater awareness of social responsibility in peace-time. As Richard Hauser says, until society expects social action from its citizens, they will continue to shirk their responsibility for social conditions by pinning blame on scapegoats. Civic training and first aid should be part of basic education; a more drastic remedy would be for everybody to contribute a compulsory short period in welfare or police work. Young people who spent a few months' civic service in being trained and then accompanying policemen on the beat might not be of much practical use, but the police would make some life-long allies.

Full enforcement of our present laws is physically impossible; consequently the police have developed a discretion in prosecuting which has expanded with the amount of legislation. This discretion forms an area of great power, which has never been properly studied or discussed: the police have appropriated from the courts many fields of mitigation. Opinion about policemen can never be far separated from feeling about the law which they are required to enforce. Citizens should be more active politically in getting legislation altered, instead of resenting its enforcement by the police. A legal code which was as simple as possible would benefit everybody. If the public through their elected representatives reformed the law into a shape which commanded general agreement and respect, a high conviction rate could operate as a real deterrent to infringement of it.

The earliest leaders of our police recognized that their ability to fulfil their functions would always depend on public approval. Today, as Mr Colin MacInnes – no apologist for the police – says, 'They are doing the difficult and dangerous job society demands without any understanding by society of what their moral and professional problems are.' The public use the police as a scapegoat for its neurotic attitude towards crime. Janus-like, we have always turned two faces towards a policeman. We expect him to be human and yet inhuman: we employ him to administer the law, and yet ask him to waive it. We resent him when he enforces a law in our own case, yet demand his dismissal when he does not elsewhere: we offer him bribes, yet denounce his corruption. We expect him to be a member of society, yet not to share its values: we admire violence, even against society itself, but condemn force by the police on our behalf. We tell the police that they are entitled to information from the public, yet we ostracize informers: we ask for crime to be eradicated, but only by the use of 'sporting' methods.

What, to end where we began, do we want the police for? Only by resolving the conflict in social values between liberty and law enforcement can we determine the paradox of the policeman's position in our future society. It is time to think clearly, and to give our police a role in which we can help and not obstruct them.

JUDGES' RULES

These Rules do not affect the principles

(a) That citizens have a duty to help a police officer to discover and apprehend offenders;

(b) That police officers, otherwise than by arrest, cannot compel any person against his will to come to or remain in any police station;

(c) That every person at any stage of an investigation should be able to communicate and to consult privately with a solicitor. This is so even if he is in custody provided that in such a case no unreasonable delay or hindrance is caused to the processes of investigation or the administration of justice by his doing so;

(d) That when a police officer who is making enquiries of any person about an offence has enough evidence to prefer a charge against that person for the offence, he should without delay cause that person to be charged or informed that he may be prosecuted for the offence;

(e) That it is a fundamental condition of the admissibility in evidence against any person, equally of any oral answer given by that person to a question put by a police officer and of any statement made by that person, that it shall have been voluntary, in the sense that it has not been obtained from him by fear of prejudice or hope of advantage, exercised or held out by a person in authority, or by oppression.

The principle set out in paragraph (e) above is overriding and applicable in all cases. Within that principle the following Rules are put forward as a guide to police officers conducting investigations. Non-conformity with these Rules may render answers and statements liable to be excluded from evidence in subsequent criminal proceedings.

RULES

I. When a police officer is trying to discover whether, or by whom, an offence has been committed he is entitled to question any person, whether suspected or not, from whom he thinks that useful information may be obtained. This is so whether or not the person in question has been taken into custody so long as he has not been charged with the offence or informed that he may be prosecuted for it.

II. As soon as a police officer has evidence which would afford reasonable grounds for suspecting that a person has committed an offence, he shall caution that person or cause him to be cautioned before putting to him any questions, or further questions, relating to that offence.

The caution shall be in the following terms:—

> 'You are not obliged to say anything unless you wish to do so but what you say may be put into writing and given in evidence.'

When after being cautioned a person is being questioned, or elects to make a statement, a record shall be kept of the time and place at which any such questioning or statement began and ended and of the persons present.

III—(a) Where a person is charged with or informed that he may be prosecuted for an offence he shall be cautioned in the following terms:—

> 'Do you wish to say anything? You are not obliged to say anything unless you wish to do so but whatever you say will be taken down in writing and may be given in evidence.'

(b) It is only in exceptional cases that questions relating to the offence should be put to the accused person after he has been charged or informed that he may be prosecuted. Such questions may be put where they are necessary for the purpose of preventing or minimising harm or loss to some other person or to the public or for clearing up an ambiguity in a previous answer or statement.

Before any such questions are put the accused should be cautioned in these terms:—

> 'I wish to put some questions to you about the offence with which you have been charged (or about the offence for which you may be prosecuted). You are not obliged to

answer any of these questions, but if you do the questions and answers will be taken down in writing and may be given in evidence.'

Any questions put and answers given relating to the offence must be contemporaneously recorded in full and the record signed by that person or if he refuses by the interrogating officer.

(c) When such a person is being questioned, or elects to make a statement, a record shall be kept of the time and place at which any questioning or statement began and ended and of the persons present.

IV. All written statements made after caution shall be taken in the following manner:—

(a) If a person says that he wants to make a statement he shall be told that it is intended to make a written record of what he says. He shall always be asked whether he wishes to write down himself what he wants to say; if he says that he cannot write or that he would like someone to write it for him, a police officer may offer to write the statement for him. If he accepts the offer the police officer shall, before starting, ask the person making the statement to sign, or make his mark to, the following:—

'I, ..., wish to make a statement. I want someone to write down what I say. I have been told that I need not say anything unless I wish to do so and that whatever I say may be given in evidence.'

(b) Any person writing his own statement shall be allowed to do so without any prompting as distinct from indicating to him what matters are material.

(c) The person making the statement, if he is going to write it himself, shall be asked to write out and sign before writing what he wants to say, the following:—

'I make this statement of my own free will. I have been told that I need not say anything unless I wish to do so and that whatever I say may be given in evidence.'

(d) Whenever a police officer writes the statement, he shall take down the exact words spoken by the person making the statement, without putting any questions other than such as may be needed to make the statement coherent, intelligible and relevant to the material matters: he shall not prompt him.

(*e*) When the writing of a statement by a police officer is finished the person making it shall be asked to read it and to make any corrections, alterations or additions he wishes. When he has finished reading it he shall be asked to write and sign or make his mark on the following Certificate at the end of the statement:—

> 'I have read the above statement and I have been told that I can correct, alter or add anything I wish. This statement is true. I have made it of my own free will.'

(*f*) If the person who has made a statement refuses to read it or to write the above mentioned Certificate at the end of it or to sign it, the senior police officer present shall record on the statement itself and in the presence of the person making it, what has happened. If the person making the statement cannot read, or refuses to read it, the officer who has taken it down shall read it over to him and ask him whether he would like to correct, alter or add anything and to put his signature or make his mark at the end. The police officer shall then certify on the statement itself what he has done.

V. If at any time after a person has been charged with, or has been informed that he may be prosecuted for an offence a police officer wishes to bring to the notice of that person any written statement made by another person who in respect of the same offence has also been charged or informed that he may be prosecuted, he shall hand to that person a true copy of such written statement, but nothing shall be said or done to invite any reply or comment. If that person says that he would like to make a statement in reply, or starts to say something, he shall at once be cautioned or further cautioned as prescribed by Rule III(*a*).

VI. Persons other than police officers charged with the duty of investigating offences or charging offenders shall, so far as may be practicable, comply with these Rules.

ADMINISTRATIVE DIRECTIONS ON INTERROGATION AND THE TAKING OF STATEMENTS

1. *Procedure generally*

(*a*) When possible statements of persons under caution should be written on the forms provided for the purpose. Police officers' notebooks should be used for taking statements only when no forms are available.

(*b*) When a person is being questioned or elects to make a statement, a record should be kept of the time or times at which during the questioning or making of a statement there were intervals or refreshment was taken. The nature of the refreshment should be noted. In no circumstances should alcoholic drink be given.

(*c*) In writing down a statement, the words used should not be translated into 'official' vocabulary; this may give a misleading impression of the genuineness of the statement.

(*d*) Care should be taken to avoid any suggestion that the person's answers can only be used in evidence against him, as this may prevent an innocent person making a statement which might help to clear him of the charge.

2. *Record of interrogation*

Rule II and Rule III(*c*) demand that a record should be kept of the following matters:—

(*a*) when, after being cautioned in accordance with Rule II, the person is being questioned or elects to make a statement—of the time and place at which any such questioning began and ended and of the persons present;

(*b*) when, after being cautioned in accordance with Rule III(*a*) or (*b*) a person is being questioned or elects to make a statement—of the time and place at which any questioning and statement began and ended and of the persons present.

In addition to the records required by these Rules full records of the following matters should additionally be kept:—

    (*a*) of the time or times at which cautions were taken, and
    (*b*) of the time when a charge was made and/or the person was arrested, and
    (*c*) of the matters referred to in paragraph 1(*b*) above.

If two or more police officers are present when the questions are being put or the statement made, the records made should be countersigned by the other officers present.

3. *Comfort and refreshment*

Reasonable arrangements should be made for the comfort and refreshment of persons being questioned. Whenever practicable both the person being questioned or making a statement and the officers asking the questions or taking the statement should be seated.

4. *Interrogation of children and young persons*

As far as practicable children (whether suspected of crime or not) should only be interviewed in the presence of a parent or guardian, or, in their absence, some person who is not a police officer and is of the same sex as the child. A child or young person should not be arrested, nor even interviewed, at school if such action can possibly be avoided. Where it is found essential to conduct the interview at school, this should be done only with the consent, and in the presence, of the head teacher, or his nominee.

5. *Interrogation of foreigners*

In the case of a foreigner making a statement in his native language:

    (*a*) The interpreter should take down the statement in the language in which it is made.
    (*b*) An official English translation should be made in due course and be proved as an exhibit with the original statement.
    (*c*) The foreigner should sign the statement at (*a*).

Apart from the question of apparent unfairness, to obtain the signature of a suspect to an English translation of what he said in a foreign language can have little or no value as evidence if the suspect disputes the accuracy of this record of his statement.

6. *Supply to accused persons of written statement of charges*

(*a*) The following procedure should be adopted whenever a charge is preferred against a person arrested without warrant for any offence:

> As soon as a charge has been accepted by the appropriate police officer the accused person should be given a written notice containing a copy of the entry in the charge sheet or book giving particulars of the offence with which he is charged. So far as possible the particulars of the charge should be stated in simple language so that the accused person may understand it, but they should also show clearly the precise offence in law with which he is charged. Where the offence charged is a statutory one, it should be sufficient for the latter purpose to quote the section of the statute which created the offence.
>
> The written notice should include some statement on the lines of the caution given orally to the accused person in accordance with the Judges' Rules after a charge has been preferred. It is suggested that the form of notice should begin with the following words:—
>
> > 'You are charged with the offence(s) shown below. You are not obliged to say anything unless you wish to do so, but whatever you say will be taken down in writing and may be given in evidence'.

(*b*) Once the accused person has appeared before the court it is not necessary to serve him with a written notice of any further charges which may be preferred. If, however, the police decide, before he has appeared before a court, to modify the charge or to prefer further charges, it is desirable that the person concerned should be formally charged with the further offence and given a written copy of the charge as soon as it is possible to do so having regard to the particular circumstances of the case. If the accused person has then been released on bail, it may not always be practicable or reasonable to prefer the new charge at once, and in cases where he is due to surrender to his bail within forty-eight hours or in other cases of difficulty it will be sufficient for him to be formally charged with the further offence and served with a written notice of the charge after he has surrendered to his bail and before he appears before the court.

7. *Facilities for defence*

(*a*) A person in custody should be allowed to speak on the telephone to his solicitor or to his friends provided that no hindrance is reasonably likely to be caused to the processes of investigation, or the administration of justice by his doing so.

He should be supplied on request with writing materials and his letters should be sent by post or otherwise with the least possible delay. Additionally, telegrams should be sent at once, at his own expense.

(*b*) Persons in custody should not only be informed orally of the rights and facilities available to them, but in addition notices describing them should be displayed at convenient and conspicuous places at police stations and the attention of persons in custody should be drawn to these notices.

THE MIRROR AND THE CROSS

The Kilmichael-Glassary Bell Shrine (National Museum of Antiquities of Scotland).